Original edition published 1985 by Casterman, Tournai
© 1985 Casterman

This edition published 1990 by Franklin Watts
© 1990 Franklin Watts

Franklin Watts
96 Leonard Street
London EC2A 4RH

ISBN: 0 86313 995 7

Editor: Kathy Keeble-Eliot

All rights reserved

Picture credits
Michel Pierre: pages 10, 11, 18L, 32, 35, 38, 39, 43, 50L, 52, 53, 54, 55, 56, 57, 62, 63, 64, 65, 67, 68, 69, 71, 72, 75, 76. Jean-Pierre Adam: pages 12, 22, 30, 34, 40, 50R, 58, 60, 61, 63. Novosti: pages 44, 45. Giraudon: pages 18R, 21. Artephot/Trela: page 42. Artephot/Nimattallah: pages 74, 75. Fulvio Roiter/Lebanese office of Tourism: pages 14/15. D.R.A.S.M.: page 73.

A CIP catalogue record for this book is available from the British Library

Printed in Portugal

THE HUMAN STORY

THE ANCIENT WORLD

Original text by Jean-Pierre Adam
Rewritten by Stewart Ross
Illustrations by Michaël Welply

FRANKLIN WATTS
London • New York • Sydney • Toronto

CONTENTS

Preface	7
The landlocked sea	8

1 The first civilisations

The island of Crete	10
Mycenae	12
The Phoenicians	14
Carthage	16
Life in Carthage	18
The Etruscans	20
Cities of the dead	22

2 The Greeks

Greek cities	24
At work in town and country	26
Athens	28
Warfare	30
Greeks overseas	32
Gods and goddesses	34
Philosophers and actors	36
The Olympic Games	38
Alexander the Great	40
The end of the Greek world	42

3 On the edge of the Greek world

The Scythians	44
The Celts	46

4 The Romans

The birth of Rome	48
The growth of the Republic	50
The age of Augustus	52
The Empire at its height	54
The best soldiers in the world	56
Life in Rome	58
Pompeii	60
The remains of the Empire	62
The fall of Rome	64
Byzantium	66

5 Researching the past

Family life in classical times	68
The travels of Ulysses	70
Diving into the past	72
Statues, paintings and pottery	74
Chronology	76
Index	77

PREFACE

There are fragments of stone all around the shores of the Mediterranean Sea. Once they were brightly painted but now they are bleached white by the sun. These broken columns are all that is left of the great civilisations which once dominated this area. And beneath the Mediterranean lie the wrecks of ancient ships which once sailed to all parts of the classical world – to Crete, Phoenicia, Carthage, Greece and Rome. Archaeologists have learned a lot about these early traders from examining the wrecks and the cargoes they once carried.

The landscape has changed dramatically since classical times. Two thousand years ago the Mediterranean coastline was densely wooded, but over the years people cut down the trees to use for fuel and building. The ancient forests have gone and what is left today is dry scrubland. There are several new types of tree and plant. Lemon trees were introduced only in late classical times, while oranges, tomatoes and cacti arrived from America over 1,000 years ago. The popular eucalyptus tree was first imported from Australia.

But we can learn a great deal about the people of classical times from the things which have survived: the buildings, paintings, statues, writing and pottery. By studying these things we can build up a picture of what life was like 2,000 years ago.

THE LANDLOCKED SEA

The Mediterranean Sea stretches 4,500 kilometres from Syria to Gibraltar. It is like a huge salt water lake which links Africa with Asia and Europe. Its name comes from Latin, the language of the Romans, and means 'in the middle of the land'.

For much of the time the sea is calm and safe for sailors, but violent gales can swiftly arise, turning the waters a stormy white. These winds have colourful local names, such as the Eltesian winds, the Sirocco, or the Mistral.

The shores of the landlocked sea are very varied. Around Greece they are rocky, in North Africa they are sandy, and the coasts of Lebanon and France are thickly wooded.

The earliest vessels to sail up and down the quiet coastal waters of the Mediterranean were prehistoric canoes. Then came sailing ships, whose crews were looking for new places to settle and new people with whom to trade. The early merchants did not use money, but exchanged goods between one port and another. Ideas and language were spread this way, too. Ships sailed from the rocky shores of Cyprus, laden with copper for making weapons and pots. Syria exported timber from her forests and the Greeks exchanged their pottery for Spanish lead. France (known then as Gaul) supplied the Mediterranean world with furs, salt meat and slaves, and in turn received olive oil and flasks of heady red wine.

The first Mediterranean civilisation was on the island of Crete, which was protected from attackers by the unpredictable sea. Later the Phoenicians became the masters of the Mediterranean. They were tireless sailors and explorers. As well as trading goods, they spread their many inventions and their alphabet around the Mediterranean shores. It is even rumoured that one of their ships was the first to sail round Africa. Their cities were later captured by invaders, but the Phoenicians never shared the secrets of their sailing skills with anyone.

Many civilisations came after the Phoenicians: the Greeks, the Etruscans and the Carthaginians. The Romans created the last great classical civilisation; they were the most powerful of all. They conquered lands all round the Mediterranean. They also defeated the pirates who had for centuries attacked trading vessels. Now the sea was safe for merchants to sail over with their cargoes of wine, oil and wheat. This made the Romans popular wherever they went. The Romans weren't afraid of anything, except perhaps the sea itself when it was stormy and dangerous.

THE FIRST CIVILISATIONS
THE ISLAND OF CRETE

The island of Crete is at the very heart of the Mediterranean, halfway between Spain and the Near East, Greece and Egypt. Neolithic farmers were the first settlers to cross the treacherous sea to its shores. They grew wheat, olives and vines, and tended flocks of sheep. The people who lived on Crete were known as Minoans.

But they were fisherfolk and traders, as well as farmers. Their small, square-sailed vessels carried fruit, bronze, oil and fabrics to countries as far apart as Syria, Greece and Egypt. For fighting and to carry passengers they built galleys, some rowed by as many as forty oarsmen. The smaller ships had square sails. The largest could take fifteen passengers as well as cargo.

Ancient Crete was ruled by priest-kings, given the title *Minos*. Remains of their magnificent palaces have been found at Mallia, Phaistos, Knossos, and Kato Zakro.

The Minoans dominated the Mediterranean for hundreds of years. Their culture spread on to the Greek mainland and their ships controlled the Aegean Sea. But in about 1400 BC the Minoan civilisation suddenly disappeared. It was probably destroyed by an earthquake and by Greek invaders. Earthquakes were quite frequent in Crete. One destroyed several palaces only 300 years before the final collapse of Minoan civilisation.

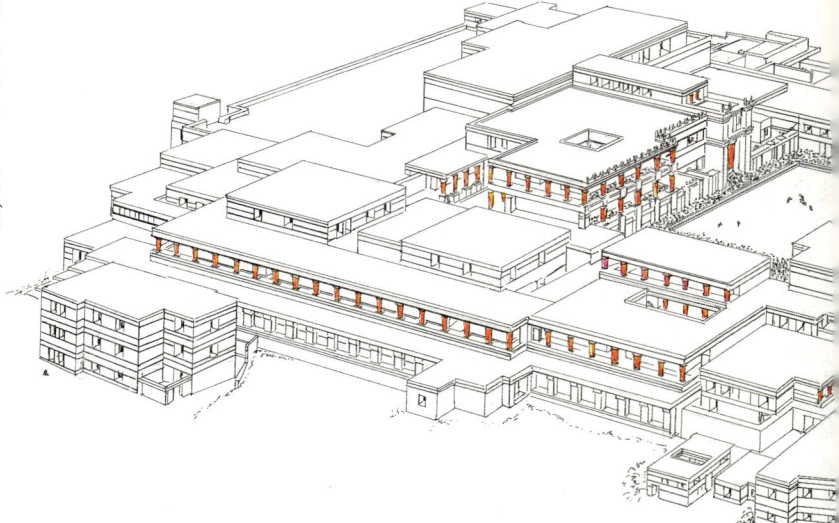

Bulls played an important part in Minoan culture. In this picture acrobats are performing stunts with an angry bull shortly before it is slain in a religious ceremony.

THE PALACE OF KNOSSOS

The royal palace of Knossos was five storeys high and contained more than 1,300 rooms. Each one was paved with tiles and covered with frescoes (wall paintings). The building was made of giant stone blocks, with red wooden columns supporting the flat roof.

There is a legend about the Minotaur who lived on Crete. It was a monster, half man and half bull, living at the centre of a maze, or labyrinth. It devoured young men and women, until it was eventually killed by the Greek hero, Theseus.

Near the palace of Knossos archaeologists have discovered urns, like the ones shown on the left. They were known as *pithoi* and were used for storing oil, grain and wine. Scholars have also found numerous clay tablets covered in writing, which cannot yet be understood.

MYCENAE

Pausanias, a Greek historian, visited the ruins of Mycenae in southern Greece almost 1,800 years ago. Even then there wasn't much left, apart from some ruined walls. But the building stones of these walls were so enormous, Pausanias said, that it would take more than two mules to move even the smallest of them.

These walls are almost all that is left of some huge fortresses the Mycenaeans built in about 1400 BC. They were strongholds against attackers. The Mycenaeans built such huge walls to frighten their enemies, as well as to protect themselves from javelins and catapults. However, they did not spend all their time behind the walls. They were an aggressive people whose armies marched to war through the famous lion gate. The king and generals went first, dressed in shining armour made of copper or bronze.

Ordinary citizens lived outside the stronghold or citadel in simple huts made of mud and wood. The kings' palaces were much simpler than those of Crete, and were at the centre of the defences. They were built round a great hall, called the *megaron*, with an open fire in the middle. When kings died they were buried in large round tombs set into the hillside.

Mycenaean civilisation was at its height in the fourteenth century BC. Then, 200 years later, a drought made some of its citizens leave the area in search of more fertile farmland. The Mycenaeans' northern neighbours invaded, and the civilisation collapsed. The people who took over were the Dorian Greeks. They destroyed the huts and fields of the conquered people, but the great fortress of Mycenae was too strong to be pulled down.

Archaeologists at Mycenae found several bodies in graves, their faces covered with gold-leaf masks. The masks enable us to see exactly what these dead Mycenaeans looked like.

THE LION GATE AT MYCENAE

The Mycenaeans built fortresses to protect themselves, but they were also attackers. Bronze-armoured kings often led bands of warriors through the Lion Gate (pictured above) on expeditions of conquest.

The Mycenaean Greeks are famous for their siege and capture of the city of Troy, led by King Agamemnon in about 1300 BC. About 500 years later Homer told their story in two epic poems, the *Iliad* and the *Odyssey*.

When a nineteenth-century archaeologist discovered skeletons covered in jewels in Mycenaean tombs, he believed that he had discovered the grave of King Agamemnon. In fact, the remains date from 300 years before Agamemnon.

THE PHOENICIANS

When Mycenaean civilisation collapsed at the end of the eleventh century the Phoenicians took over as the dominant Mediterranean power. They became a major trading nation, exporting wine, wheat, oil and a famous purple dye. A story is told that this dye was first discovered when a sheep dog broke open a murex shell on the beach. This released a bright purple stain, which the Phoenicians were quick to use as an excellent dye for colouring their fabrics.

The Phoenicians set up trading posts and shipyards all around the shores of the Mediterranean. One reason why they were so successful was that they lived midway between Egypt and Mesopotamia. These were two of the wealthiest regions in the ancient world; they needed to buy and sell goods all over the Mediterranean. The Phoenicians carried much of their trade for them.

By about 700 BC the Phoenicians had bases on the African coast in Libya, Morocco and Tunisia, on the islands of Malta, Sicily and Sardinia, and even as far away as Spain. They chose bases carefully. They had to have sheltered harbours and sloping shores so that boats could easily be pulled from the sea for repairs. The towns also had to have good communications inland with farmers, merchants and craftsmen. The Phoenicians did not use money, but exchanged goods. They were skilled as shipbuilders, goldsmiths and glassmakers.

Except for a few walls and tombs, no Phoenician architecture remains today. But we know that the Phoenicians were excellent builders, because King Solomon employed them to make his new temple in Jerusalem.

Phoenician ships were well made from cedar wood and pine, and had square woven sails. They were steered by oars at the stern, and sailed the length and breadth of the Mediterranean. Their chief ports (Byblos, Berytus, Tyre and Sidon) are in what is now modern Lebanon.

THE WEALTH OF THE PHOENICIANS

These bronze and gold leaf figures, uncovered at Byblos in Phoenicia, show the wealth and skill of Phoenician craftsmen. The Old Testament prophet Ezekiel mentions the riches which the Phoenicians built up. He was very impressed with their skill as sailors and traders.

The first writing used by the people of the Near East was cuneiform (wedge-shaped writing) or hieroglyphics, which were really simplified pictures. These were very difficult to read and write, for there were between 300 and 800 different signs to learn. The first modern alphabet came from Syria in about 1500 BC. This alphabet didn't have any vowels, only consonants. It is still used in Arabic and Hebrew.

Five hundred years later the Phoenicians developed their own twenty-two character alphabet, which can be seen on the tomb of King Ahiram, shown on the left. It was slowly adopted by all the Greek world and modified over the centuries. Vowels were added, and it gradually developed into the alphabet which you are reading now.

CARTHAGE

There is a legend that Carthage was founded by Dido, a Phoenician princess, whose cruel brother forced her to flee with some followers. After a long voyage they reached what is now Tunisia in North Africa. The local inhabitants granted Dido as much land as she could cover with a bull's hide. So she craftily cut a bull's hide into thin strips, laid them out round a huge area, and proceeded to build a fortress. The settlement rapidly developed into the flourishing port of Carthage.

This story has been made famous by the Roman poet Virgil in his poem, the *Aeneid*. However, modern archaeologists have confirmed that there is some truth in the legend, for Carthage was definitely founded in about 800 BC by Phoenician settlers.

Carthage was built on a rocky outcrop, protected in the west by a semicircle of hills. The Citadel of Byrsa stood on the highest peak. The port had two harbours joined by a canal. One was for warships, the other for trading ships. Ships brought precious metals, iron, lead, copper and tin to the commercial harbour. The city's exports were mainly ivory, rare hardwoods, cereals and olive oil. Carthage was at the centre of a great trading empire, with colonies all over the western Mediterranean. At one time it even controlled the Pillars of Hercules, now known as the Straits of Gibraltar, which gave it some control over trade in the Atlantic as well.

Carthage paid for two famous voyages of exploration. Himilco sailed out of the Mediterranean and up the coast of Europe, past Spain and France, as far as the British Isles. He was looking for tin and lead, two metals which were in short supply in the Mediterranean. The most famous voyage was made by Hanno. He turned south when he left the Mediterranean and made his way along the African shore. He took his fleet of sixty ships as far as the Gulf of Guinea before turning back.

Carthage's period of greatness came to an end when it came into conflict with Rome. Carthage and Rome fought three wars, known as the Punic Wars. The first was fought between 264 and 241 BC. It came to a close when neither side was able to gain the advantage. Carthage was defeated in the second war (218-201 BC) but managed to recover her strength, rebuild her fleet and army, and attack the Romans again. But finally the Romans proved too strong. At the end of the last war Carthage was destroyed and priests declared that the city would be cursed for ever. However, it later recovered and became a wealthy city again within the Roman empire. Its population numbered over 300,000.

Some of the ships using Carthage's port had crews of over 210 oarsmen. They were controlled from the admiralty building, which stood on a rocky island in the middle of the harbour, by a system of lights and sounds. Warships could be repaired out of sight on covered slipways.

For storing wine, oil or cereals the Carthaginians used large pointed jars, known as *amphorae*. One is shown on the left.

The picture below on the right shows the mighty town and harbours of Carthage. The picture on the left shows all that is left today: a few ruins scattered along the shores of shallow, sandy pools.

LIFE IN CARTHAGE

Carthage was at its most powerful in the third century BC. Its population of over 100,000 was made up of people from all over the Mediterranean: Phoenicians, Numidians, Libyans, Iberians and Greeks. There were also slaves, mainly from Africa, whom the Carthaginians sometimes freed and permitted to live as ordinary citizens.

The city was governed by a council of 104 magistrates who were elected by the citizens of Carthage. Their generals, who were also elected, faced execution if their armies were defeated. When the Carthaginians failed to defeat the Romans in the first Punic War, four of their generals were crucified. The generals were always of aristocratic birth, but the men they commanded were mercenaries or professional soldiers, who came from all over the Mediterranean and were paid to fight.

Excavations at Carthage have told us a lot about how its people lived. The rich lived in comfortable villas, along paved and well drained roads. The poorer citizens lived in blocks of flats, sometimes six storeys high, which were jammed together along narrow streets. In such conditions fire was a serious and constant hazard: at least twice Carthage was badly damaged by fire.

The city was surrounded by rich farmland, which was tended with great skill. Carthaginians were famous throughout the Mediterranean world as excellent farmers. One of their landowners, called Mago, wrote down all he knew about the skill of farming in a famous book, *Treatise on Agriculture*. It was twenty-eight volumes long. When the Romans finally captured Carthage in 146 BC they burned the city to the ground. Before they did so, however, their commander made sure that Mago's treatise was safe in Roman hands. He did not want to see so valuable a work destroyed in the flames.

This model of a bather in a hip bath, pouring water over herself from a bowl, was found in excavations at Carthage.

Hannibal was born in Carthage and was an outstanding military leader. He led his army and a herd of war elephants over the Alps into Italy in 218 BC to attack the Romans. He crushed the Romans at Cannae, but he was eventually forced to retreat to Carthage, where he was defeated in 202 BC. Later Hannibal committed suicide rather than surrender.

THE SACRIFICE OF CHILDREN

In a ceremony known as Moloch, the Carthaginians sacrificed young children to Baal-Hammon, lord of the sun, their god of warmth. The dead child's ashes were then placed in an urn and buried, often under an obelisk like the one shown here. Sometimes parents could save their babies by sacrificing a young animal instead.

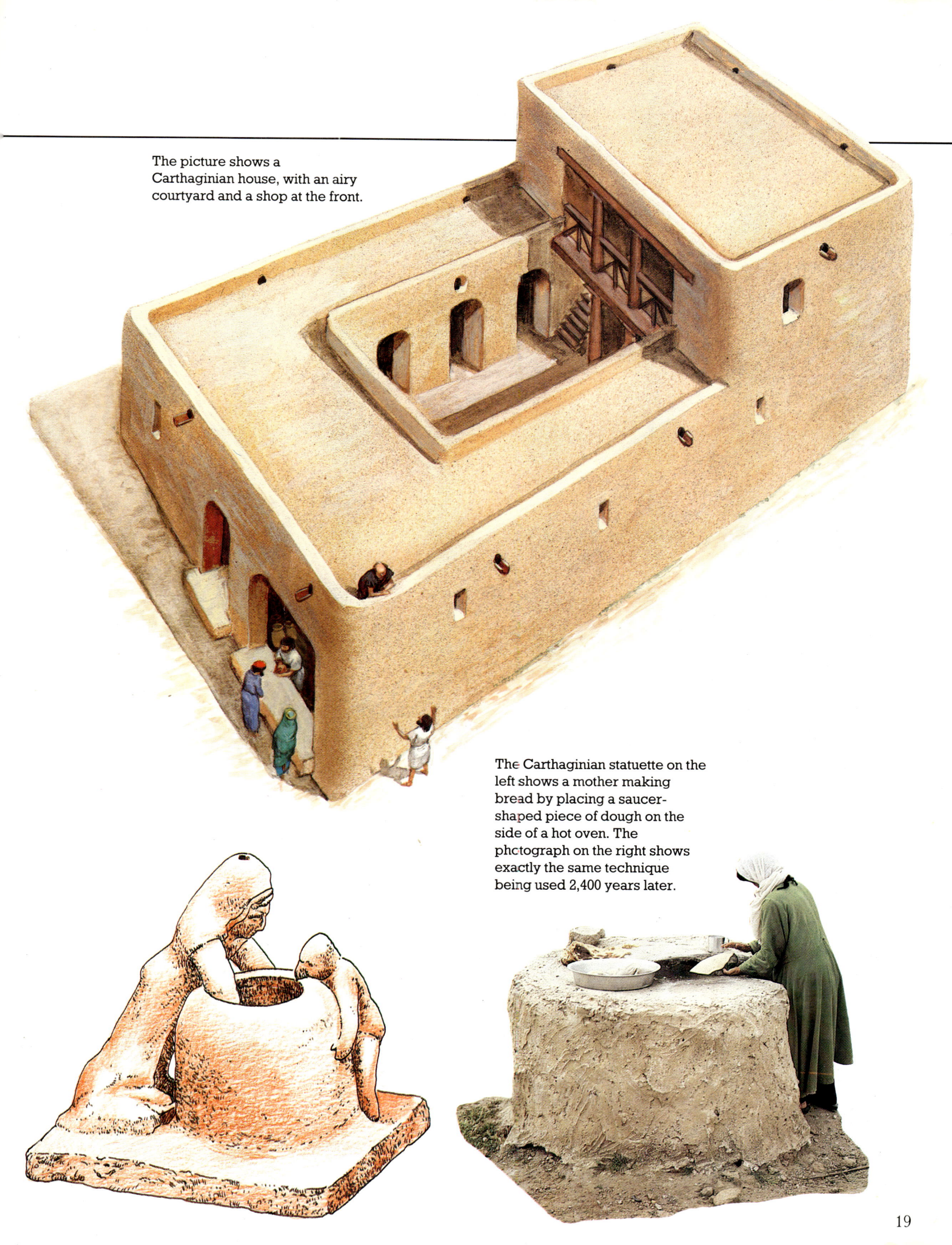

The picture shows a Carthaginian house, with an airy courtyard and a shop at the front.

The Carthaginian statuette on the left shows a mother making bread by placing a saucer-shaped piece of dough on the side of a hot oven. The photograph on the right shows exactly the same technique being used 2,400 years later.

THE ETRUSCANS

The Etruscans came from Asia Minor and were the first to build cities in Italy. They developed a sophisticated culture of their own long before the Romans became powerful.

The first Etruscan cities were in northern Italy in what is now Tuscany. Each city was ruled by its own king, but eventually these kings joined together and conquered land to the east and the south. They moved into Latium, where they founded Rome, and down into Campania. They knew how to make excellent weapons from iron, which helped their success in wars.

We do not know much about how the Etruscans lived, for their towns have almost all disappeared, and we cannot decipher their writing. But remains in the town of Marzabotto, south of modern Bologna, give us some idea of Etruscan city life. Roads were built in straight lines, crossing each other at right angles. Beside them stood large rectangular buildings. Most of the shops and workshops faced on to the main street. The houses were a series of rooms around a courtyard with its own well. On a low hill there were three temples whose walls were made of clay and wood.

The wealthy aristocratic families which dominated Etruscan society lived idle lives on their huge country estates. They passed their time in feasting and being entertained by their own musicians, athletes and artists.

In the sixth century BC the Etruscans were at their most powerful. However they came into conflict with the Greeks who were setting up settlements in southern Italy. The Etruscans made an alliance with the Carthaginians, who had a magnificent navy of galleys. In about 540 BC the Etruscans and their allies put to sea with a fleet of 120 ships, but in a gigantic battle they were defeated by a mere sixty Greek galleys. After the fight the Greeks withdrew because they feared another attack. A hundred years later the Etruscans were attacked by two Greek fleets. Shortly afterwards Samnite raiders from the Apennine mountains in the north drove the Etruscans out of Campania. Then came the Romans, who seized city after city, in the third century BC, and destroyed the remains of Etruscan civilisation for ever.

The Etruscans were famous throughout the Mediterranean world for their beautiful mirrors, jewellery and ornaments, and their powerful weaponry. They were skilled craftsmen, and used minerals from nearby mines.

Judging by the paintings that have been found, the Etruscans seem to have been keen on feasts and parties. Women took part in these festivities. They were treated equally in many other aspects of life – something that didn't often happen in classical times.

As this statuette of a war chariot shows, the Etruscans were highly skilled at working in bronze.

CITIES OF THE DEAD

Etruscan necropolises, or cities of the dead, were burial sites. Many have been excellently preserved, and from them we can learn a good deal about Etruscan life.

At an Etruscan funeral, relatives and friends gathered together, and there was music and dancing. It was more like a party than a funeral. The body was then taken to its grave on a cart, followed by women mourners chanting and wailing.

The Etruscans believed that if a dead person was given human blood, then he or she would be guaranteed eternal life. So they organised brutal fights between prisoners, or simply threw their captives into an arena with wild animals. The unhappy victims were torn to pieces by the beasts. Blood from the victims was then given to the dead person. One Etruscan tomb painting shows a man with a sack over his head, armed with only a stick, confronting an angry dog. The master of the games is urging the dog to attack the man.

The tombs of the most wealthy families were like houses dug out of solid rock. The rooms were decorated with paintings or carvings of everyday objects, such as furniture and weapons. Beds for the corpses, each with a chair at one end, were arranged along the walls.

The Etruscans believed that a winged spirit accompanied the souls of the dead on their final journey to a place of eternal rest. Carvings show the dead travelling on foot, on horseback, in a chariot, or even by boat.

Women were regarded almost as highly as men in Etruscan society. On tombs, the names of both the dead person's mother and father were written. This was unusual in classical times. Etruscan women played a full part in most aspects of life. They attended games, took part in ceremonies, and participated in politics.

THE NECROPOLIS AT CERVETERI

Some remarkable cemeteries have been discovered outside Cerveteri. Hundreds of buried tombs, built like houses, stretch in long rows of mounds across the countryside, like the one shown above. Although the actual town of Cerveteri was destroyed and rebuilt many times, there is nothing left of it today.

The Etruscans were superstitious people. This sarcophagus, or stone coffin, was found in a tomb at Cerveteri. It shows a husband and wife enjoying a meal together on a couch. The sculpture was made to ensure that the couple enjoyed such meals in the after-life. Other religious customs included priests reading the future in the entrails (internal organs) of animals, in the flight of birds, or even in flashes of lightning.

This famous tomb at Cerveteri, called the Tomb of the Reliefs, was carved out of rock in the fourth century BC. A steep stair leads into it. In the walls are fourteen alcoves for funeral couches. Most of the floor space is taken up with hollow benches for the bodies. The walls and pillars are decorated with replicas of the deceased's property. Inscriptions on the walls tell us it was built for the Matuna family.

THE GREEKS
GREEK CITIES

In the twelfth century BC the Mycenaean civilisation in southern Greece collapsed. The Greek world then passed through a Dark Age when little contact was made with the outside world. But gradually the Greeks learned how to make farming tools and weapons from iron. They became skilled farmers and soldiers, and gradually their wealth and importance returned.

City states grew up, with their own kings. Each city-state was dominated by an acropolis (stronghold) on which temples and sanctuaries were built. Craftsmen became skilled in making things out of stone, bronze and precious metals, and by the fifth century BC Greek culture was beginning its golden era, the classical period.

A Greek city-state, or *polis*, included not just a city, but also the surrounding villages and countryside. Quite often a city's defences were built to enclose some agricultural land, so that those inside could feed themselves during times of siege. A thick-walled fortress stood at the centre of the fortifications.

At the heart of every city lay the *agora*, or public square. This is where people met, and where all the main public buildings could be found. These included the council chamber, the court, and the temples. In and around the square itself there were shops and stalls. Other important buildings that stood near the city centre were the gymnasium, which was used as a school as well as for fitness, public bath houses, a theatre and a sports stadium.

Each *polis* was run in a different way. In Sparta all power was in the hands of the Spartan citizens, and no one else had any rights. The population of Athens was divided into three groups. The largest was the citizens, of whom there were about 150,000 in the fifth century BC. Thirty-five thousand metics made up the second group. They were foreigners who had come to live in Athens. They had to pay taxes and serve in the army for a time. The last group were the slaves. There were about 80,000 of them, including women and children. They had no rights and were treated merely as pieces of property.

From about the fifth century BC, many city-states were run by an assembly of male citizens. Members of these assemblies were then elected to positions in the government. This idea, that the people should control their own affairs, is the origin of democracy (*demos* is the Greek word for 'people').

Money was first used in Greece in the seventh century BC. By the sixth century BC, gold, silver and bronze coins were seen throughout the Greek world. The largest unit of currency was the *talenton*. Each *talenton* weighed about 38 kg and was divided into sixty *minai*. One *mina* was made up of 100 *drachma*, and each *drachma* was divided into six *oboloi*. Some cities like Athens used money early on, but the Spartans were very slow to start making coins of their own.

24

Olive oil was indispensable in the ancient world. It was used for cooking, burning in lamps, cleaning, in cosmetics, and as an offering to the gods. Olive trees were so highly prized that anyone caught destroying one was severely punished.

All the early Mediterranean civilisations were based on slavery. Slaves were either citizens who had lost their money, were prisoners of war or the children of slaves. The sort of life a slave led depended on who owned him. Most house slaves, for example, were better off than those who worked in the mines. Slaves could buy their freedom or it could be given to them by a kindly master.

AT WORK IN TOWN AND COUNTRY

Hesiod, a poet of the eighth century BC and Xenophion, an historian, both wrote about life in the Greek countryside. What they saw was similar but Xenophion lived 400 years later than Hesiod. Things hadn't changed much in those 400 years. Much of what they described in ancient times can still be seen in Greece today.

There were three types of farmer. The first owned a little land and did most of the work on it himself. The second type was the larger landowner, who merely supervised the work of others. The third was the owner of vast estates, who lived in the town and employed a manager to supervise his estates.

Greek farming methods were very simple. Ploughing was done by mules or oxen. The wheat was cut with a sickle and was trampled on the threshing floor by animals to separate the grain from the straw. Flour was made by grinding the grain with a pestle and mortar, or in a hand-driven stone mill. Fruit and vegetables were grown in plots around the farmhouse, and bees were kept for honey. Although cattle and horses were rare, the Greeks tended large flocks of sheep and goats. They kept donkeys and mules for the heavy work.

Greek farmers could make for themselves almost everything they needed. They grew their own food, made their own clothes from wool, and made most of their own farm implements. But they could not make large and expensive pieces of machinery. These had to be bought from the neighbouring towns with money the farmers had made from selling their produce.

In the towns craftsmen worked near the *agora*. People with the same skill often lived near each other. Potters, for example, gathered in the Keramaikos district.

The Greeks were famous for their pottery and their metalwork. They used potter's wheels to make fine, evenly shaped vases from clay. Metal goods were made in forges. These had a blazing fire, an anvil and a bucket of water into which hot iron was plunged when it had been shaped. Sometimes metal was cast into a special design by using a mould. This needed a furnace hot enough to melt metal. Household goods and weapons were made from iron and bronze.

Other craftsmen worked in the towns, making goods from leather and ivory, stone and woollen cloth. One of the most important workers was the armourer. The Greeks were a warlike people, always needing tough armour to protect their soldiers. Iron was the strongest material but as it went rusty, bronze (made of copper mixed with small quantities of other metals) was more popular.

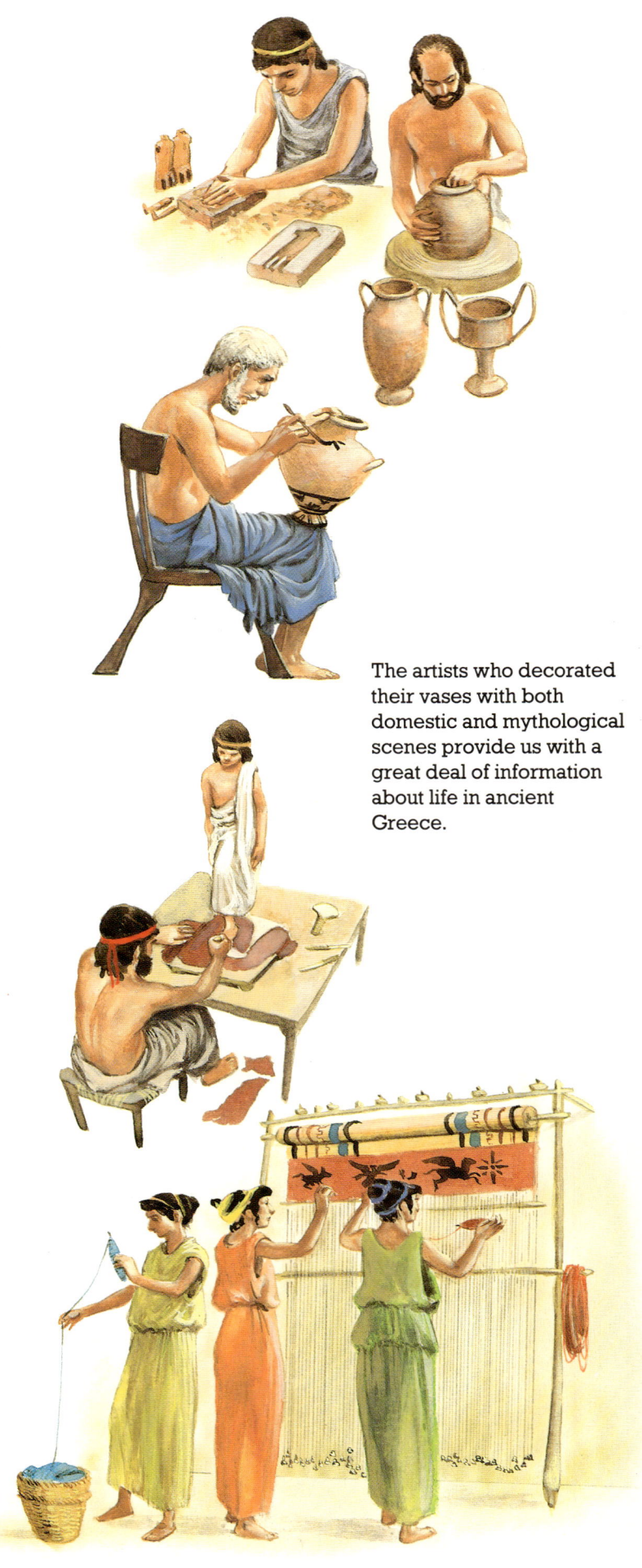

The artists who decorated their vases with both domestic and mythological scenes provide us with a great deal of information about life in ancient Greece.

26

HOW GREEK CITIES WERE RUN

The Greeks were proud of their well-ordered cities, and employed magistrates (*astynomoi*) to ensure that:
● festivals were orderly, and religious monuments were regularly cleaned
● the streets were swept and well maintained
● rubbish and sewage was properly disposed of
● the water supply and drinking fountains were not polluted, and that animals did not drink from the same sources as people
● public parks and squares were not built on.

Fines were imposed on those who broke the regulations.

ATHENS

There are many stories about the beginning of Athens, but in fact the city grew up gradually around its acropolis. Athens had many natural advantages. It was near the Aegean Sea, and therefore in a good position for trade and fishing. The surrounding farmland was good for growing food and feeding animals. There was silver from the mines at Laurion for making coins. The marble from local Mount Pendelikon was ideal for building the city's beautiful houses and temples.

In the fifth century BC there were 250,000 people living in Athens. Every male citizen over the age of twenty was allowed to attend the *ecclesia* (assembly). The members of the *ecclesia* decided the laws of Athens. So by attending its meetings, all men could have a say in the running of the government.

The Senate was an assembly of 500, chosen by lot from all men over the age of thirty. It made sure that the laws made by the *ecclesia* were carried out. Each day, an *epistates*, a sort of Prime Minister, was chosen by lot from the *ecclesia*. So every citizen had a chance of one day becoming Prime Minister! In reality, the most powerful figures were the ten men in charge of religious festivals, and the ten generals (*strategoi*), who commanded the navy, summoned the *ecclesia*, and dealt with foreign countries.

Athenian judges (*heliasts*) were also chosen by lot. Trials could last for only a day, at the end of which the judges voted the accused guilty or not guilty. If a prisoner was found guilty by a narrow margin of votes, then he could choose his own form of punishment. The famous philosopher Socrates mocked the court by choosing a ridiculous punishment, and so he was ordered to commit suicide by drinking hemlock.

The greatest Athenian military achievement was their defeat of the Persians on land, at the battle of Marathon in 490 BC, and in a naval battle at Salamis in 480 BC. However, the great power of Athens ended in 404 BC when it was defeated by Sparta and its allies.

The Acropolis of Athens was a collection of magnificent buildings. The entrance was a marble hall, with five doors. To the north there was a picture gallery, and to the south lay a temple dedicated to Athena the Triumphant. Near the entrance hall was a gigantic wooden statue of the goddess, 9 m high, which could be seen by sailors on the coast. To the right stood the immense Parthenon, the main temple of Athena. Nearby was the Erechtheum. In the courtyard of this building a sacred olive tree grew, supposedly placed there by the goddess herself.

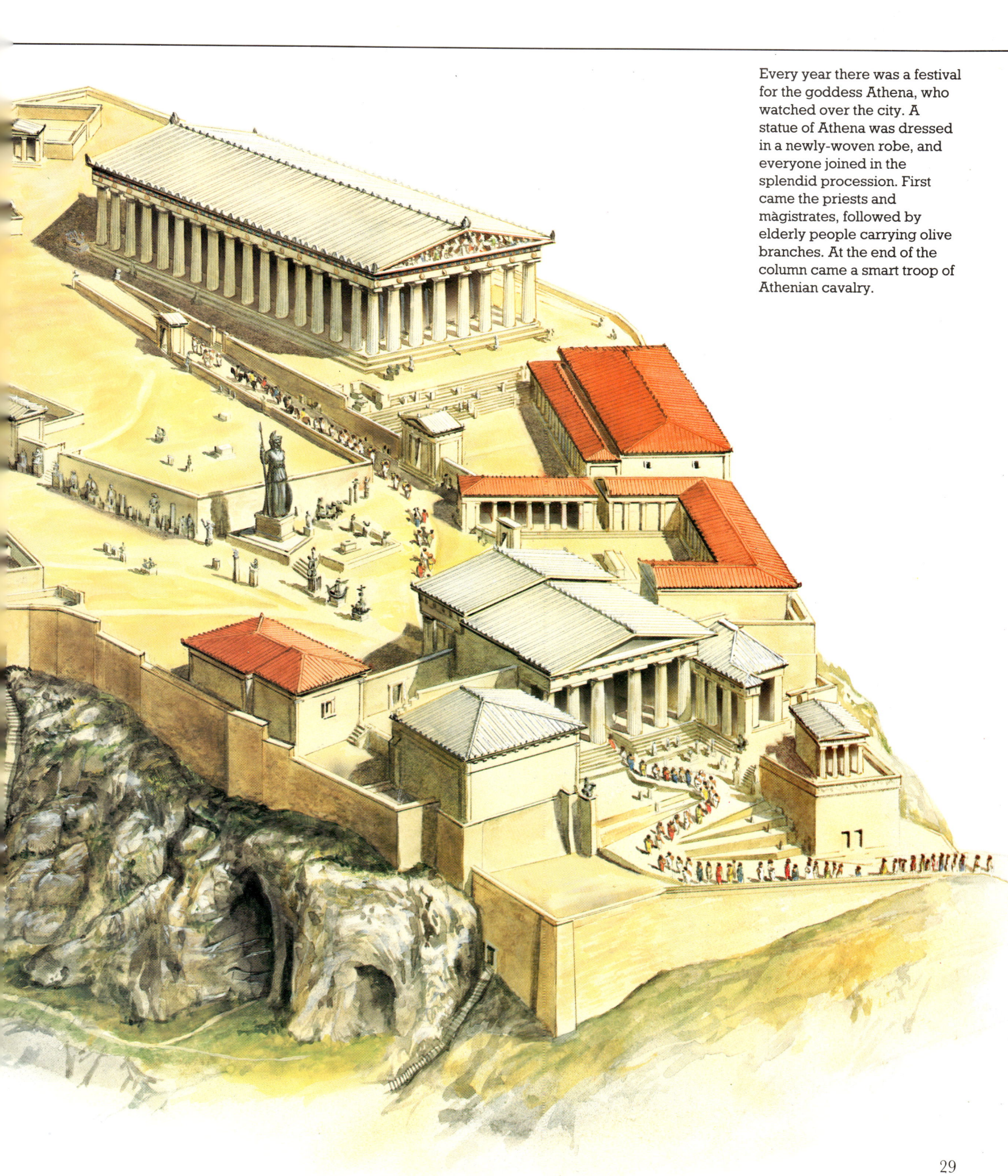

Every year there was a festival for the goddess Athena, who watched over the city. A statue of Athena was dressed in a newly-woven robe, and everyone joined in the splendid procession. First came the priests and magistrates, followed by elderly people carrying olive branches. At the end of the column came a smart troop of Athenian cavalry.

WARFARE

The Greeks seemed to be almost constantly at war, either against their neighbours or with one another. Athenians between the ages of eighteen and sixty could be asked at any time to join the army. Boys began their training early, at about the age of twelve. They went to special schools where they were made fit and strong by gymnastics and wrestling, and where they learned to handle the discus and javelin. They were tested against each other at games in the local stadium and might later represent their city in lavish athletic sports.

During the first two years after school young men were taught to use shields, spears, swords and the bow. They were also taught how to put on a helmet, breastplate and other pieces of armour. Bows were not always a fashionable weapon. But when in the fifth century BC the soldiers of Athens saw how skilfully the Persians used them, bows were re-introduced. They were not the long bows which Welsh and English archers used in the Middle Ages, but shorter weapons which could be fired more quickly.

After two years' training and a spell on garrison duty, a man became a frontline soldier. He was known as a *hoplite*, from the word *hoplon*, meaning shield. After the age of fifty soldiers joined the reserves, to be called up when needed.

When the *hoplites* moved into battle they were accompanied by slaves and poor citizens. They joined in the fighting with a variety of weapons, such as slings, which threw pieces of clay or metal with deadly accuracy.

The strictest training for *hoplites* was given in Sparta, where military skill was very highly prized. Boys were taken from their mothers at the age of seven. From then on all their education was designed to make them into effective soldiers. All schools were run by the state and pupils had to remain at them until the age of sixteen. Culture was almost completely ignored. They learned to obey orders, overcome exhaustion, and win battles. Without doubt, the Spartans were the most feared soldiers in Greece.

To make them tough, from the age of twelve Spartan men were permitted to wear only a cloak. They were severely whipped for any mistake, no matter how small. Discipline grew stricter year by year. The soldiers were allowed no private lives of their own, and they had to take all meals with their comrades. Their food consisted of barley cake, olives and onions and they had to learn to hunt or steal in order to get enough to eat. On feast days they were given a special treat: a black broth, made of pork and blood, mixed with vinegar, salt and spices.

Most of a Greek army was made up of the *hoplites*. Each man was armed with a metal-tipped spear, a sword and dagger. The Spartans wore red tunics, so that the enemy could not tell when they were wounded. For protection each *hoplite* carried a round shield, and wore armour consisting of a helmet, a cuirass covering the body, and greaves on the legs.

There were only a few cavalry, because horses were expensive to buy and take care of. Their riders, armed with swords or spears, rode without saddles.

An army fought standing close together. The enemy was faced with a wall of spears which was difficult to break.

The Athenians also had a large navy of triremes (ships equipped with three rows of oars) based at Piraeus, a port on the Aegean Sea.

GREEKS OVERSEAS

After about 750 BC many Greeks left their over-populated cities to live in foreign countries. Over a 200-year period they set up colonies scattered all over the Mediterranean world: in Sicily, Spain and southern Italy, and even in areas as remote as Gaul (modern France) and on the shores of the Black Sea. The earliest colonies were those set up in Asia Minor. These new colonies governed themselves, but many Greeks who lived there still spoke the same language and followed the same customs as the Greeks who lived on the mainland of Greece.

Later, in the fourth century BC, the Greeks established colonies as far east as Egypt, Syria and what is now Iran. Many of these were founded as a result of the conquests of the mightiest Greek warrior, Alexander the Great. Greek culture (or Hellenism, as it was called at that time) stretched from one side of the Mediterranean to the other.

Some of the more famous colonies were Massilia (the present-day Marseilles), founded by settlers from Asia Minor, and Syracuse, established by Greeks from Corinth. They governed themselves but they were on friendly terms with Athens. They set up colonies of their own around the Mediterranean.

Not all the Greek colonies were self-governing. Some, known as *klerouchiai*, were supervised by a city-state on the Greek mainland. Athens established this type of colony on the island of Euboea, then on various islands in the Aegean Sea. Land was allocated to the city's poorest citizens by a system of drawing lots. This prevented the rich from taking advantage of the Athenian expansion, and was a way of helping people make new lives for themselves.

Before setting out, the colonists asked the advice of an oracle; speaking through the priests or priestesses the gods told the colonists the best place for the new city to be built and the best time to leave their homeland. The most famous oracles were at Dodona and Delphi.

People decided to move abroad for many different reasons. Some were poor, and thought life would be better in a new place. Others were forced to leave their cities when they disagreed with the government.

Settlers took with them their belongings, animals, and a sacred fire, which was used to start the first fire in the new city. When they had arrived safely, they made sacrifices to the gods, and then began planning their new city.

GREATER GREECE

There was so much Greek influence in Sicily and southern Italy that the region became known as *Magna Graecia* or Greater Greece. The cities that sprang up here had fine public buildings and temples in the classical style, such as the Temple of Concord at Agrigento in Sicily, shown above.

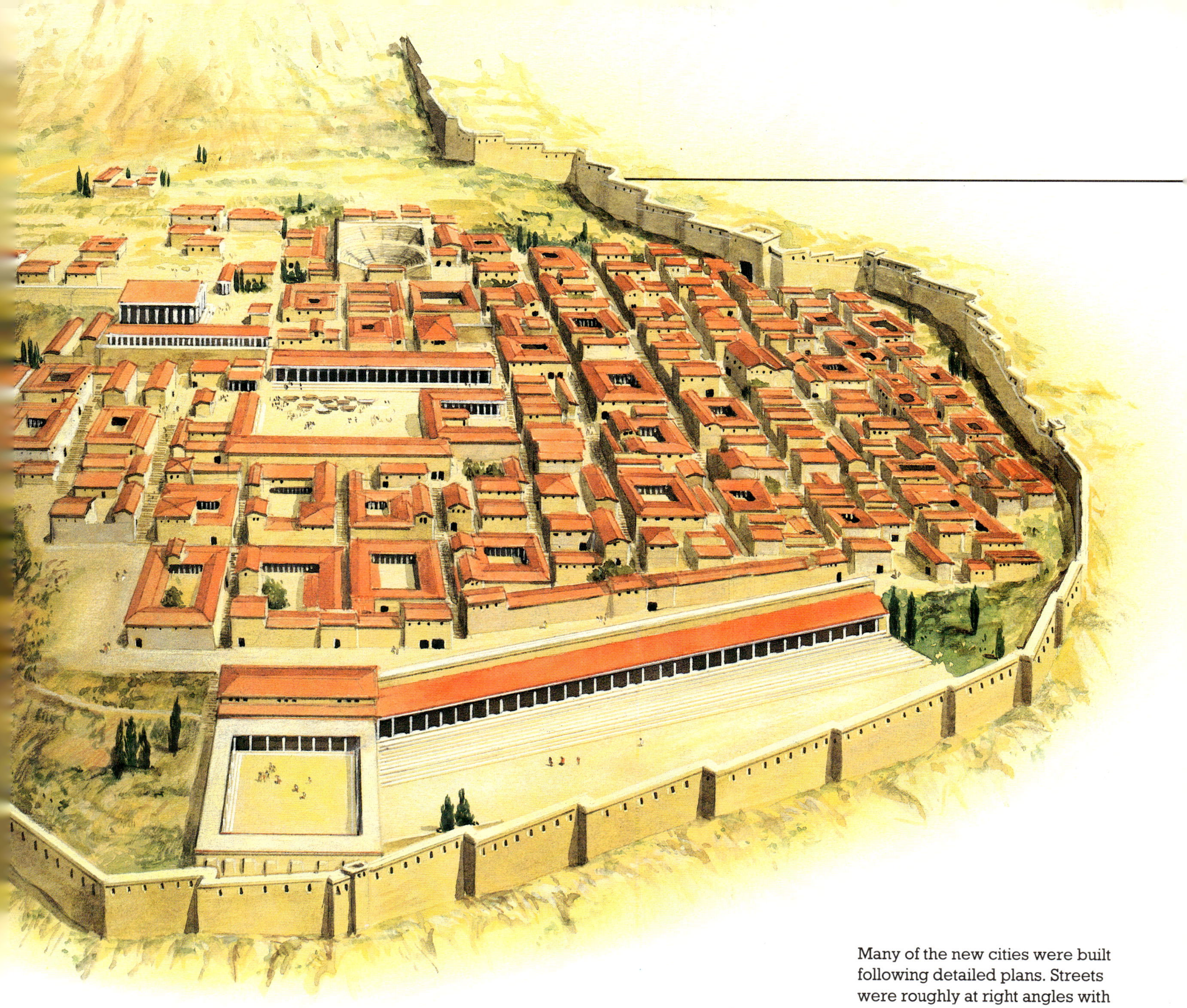

Many of the new cities were built following detailed plans. Streets were roughly at right angles with each other, like the ones in the picture, so that buildings could be arranged in an orderly fashion. Sometimes streets were named after gods or characters from Greek mythology.

The colony of Massilia (now Marseilles, in France) is supposed to have been founded by a local princess who married a Greek sailor. The wealth of the town came from buying and selling tin, silver, amber and produce from farms.

The coin on the left is from Massilia.

The ships that carried Greek settlers to their new homes, like the one in the picture, were about 15 m long, square-sailed and steered by huge paddles. They were made from many types of tree: cypress, cedar, oak, elm and flexible pine for the planking.

GODS AND GODDESSES

The earliest Mediterranean civilisations worshipped a range of mother figures who were responsible for the prosperity of agriculture. This changed when invaders called Achaens brought a number of gods with them. The female deities lost much of their following, and by the time of Mycenaean civilisation male figures were worshipped throughout Greece.

The Greeks believed in many gods. The chief god, and father of many other gods, was Zeus. He ruled the heavens. He had two brothers: Poseidon who ruled the seas, and Hades, who governed the underworld.

The Greeks believed that the gods and goddesses looked like human beings, except for Pan, who was half man and half goat. Greek mythology is about the lives of the gods and what happened to the ordinary men and women who met them. The Greeks made their gods and goddesses very human in appearance and behaviour. Much of what they were supposed to have done was very cruel, but it was accepted by the Greeks because they believed that human standards did not apply to the gods. Woe betide any mere mortal who tried to question the ways of the gods!

In about 800 BC it became customary to build temples and shrines to local gods. The most popular gods were Dionysus, the god of wine and fertility, and Aesculapius, the god of healing. The favourite goddesses were Demeter and Kore, who looked after crops and harvests. By the fifth century BC all Greeks worshipped the same gods, and many visited the famous temples at Athens, Olympia, Delphi, Delos and Dodona.

By the seventh century BC Delphi had become one of the most popular religious centres in Greece. Every city-state built a treasury there where its offerings could be stored. (One is shown in the picture above.)

The gods and goddesses were supposed to live on the cloud-capped summit of Mount Olympus. The most powerful was Zeus, who spoke with the voice of thunder. Poseidon, the sea god, who controlled storms and earthquakes, was much feared, as was Hades in his kingdom of the underworld. Kinder behaviour was expected from Apollo, the god of beauty, who also offered advice through the oracle at Delphi. Athena, goddess of the arts and wisdom, and Aphrodite, the goddess of love, were both well liked. The food and drink of the gods was said to be ambrosia and nectar.

Zeus King of the gods

Hera Zeus's sister and wife

Hermes messenger of the gods

Hephaestus god of fire, son of Zeus

Aphrodite goddess of love and beauty

Athena goddess of wisdom, the arts and war

The first centres of Greek religion were springs and woods which a god was said to visit. People brought to the gods offerings of food, gold and silver. Later, in the sixth century BC, they began to build temples on these sites. These were often vast buildings decorated with columns, paintings and sculpture. Inside burned a special fire, and a statue of the god or goddess was placed in the main hall. The most famous of these was one of the wonders of the world: the statue of Zeus at Olympia. This gigantic image, shown in the picture, was made of ivory, and clothed in pure gold.

BURIAL
When someone died in ancient Greece, the body was washed, wrapped in white sheets, and quickly buried by night. A coin was placed in the mouth of every dead body. This was to pay Charon, the ferryman who carried the departed to the underworld.

Graves were marked with marble columns, like the one shown below.

Poseidon god of the sea

Apollo god of beauty, music and prophecy

Artemis goddess of hunting

Hestia goddess of the hearth

Demeter goddess of harvest

Ares god of war, son of Zeus

35

PHILOSOPHERS AND ACTORS

The ancient Greeks wanted to know more and more about the world they lived in. They enjoyed discussing things like love and death, even at banquets. They also liked watching plays, which told them about other people's lives. The philosophers and actors of ancient Greece tried, in different ways, to explain the world and people's behaviour.

Philosophers were wise men who believed that there was a logical explanation for everything, even earthquakes and eclipses. Thales, a philosopher who lived in the sixth century BC, believed that everything in the universe started from water, but he made a fool of himself one day when he accidentally fell down a well! Nevertheless, he is remembered as having worked out when an eclipse of the sun would take place in 585 BC.

These early philosophers were trying to find a way of explaining how the universe worked. Before their time, when people did not understand something they said that it must be the work of the gods. Philosophers gave different answers, based on logic. Pythagoras was another famous thinker living at this time. He believed that all things in the universe were in harmony with each other. He made famous discoveries in geometry and music, and he believed that when a person died, his soul passed into a new, living body.

Socrates, Plato, and Aristotle were three philosophers who made great reputations for their ideas about life and politics. They didn't believe in gods and goddesses. But such thinking offended many people. Socrates was made to commit suicide by drinking poison because he said that the gods of Athens didn't exist. One of his best-known pupils was Plato. He carried on the traditions of his master and in turn passed them on to men like Aristotle.

The Greeks loved plays. During the festival of Dionysus, the god of wine and pleasure, the whole of Athens packed into the amphitheatres at Athens and Epidaurus. The poor were even given some money so that they could go. Crowds of 15,000 citizens were entertained by drama and poetry from sunrise to sunset. Sometimes five plays were performed in one day. The lively audience brought their own food and drink, and joined in the performances with cheers and boos.

At first, in the sixth century BC, the shows consisted simply of a chorus telling the story of Dionysus. Later, other tales from Greek mythology were related, and actors appeared on the stage. This is how drama, as we know it today, was born.

Philosophers taught in the gymnasia (special schools), walking about and talking to their pupils. Plato, the philosopher, set up a school of higher learning in a park called Academus on the outskirts of Athens. This is where the word 'academy' comes from.

Greek theatres were semi-circular and set into hillsides. The area nearest the audience, where the chorus performed, was called the orchestra. Behind this was a raised stage for the main actors. At the back was a wall fitted with movable panels, on which the scenery was painted. Theatres were open air, but they were so well designed that the whole audience could hear every word that was spoken.

The actors, who were always men, wore masks, and spoke or sang in verse, while the chorus commented on what was going on.

The most famous writers of tragedy were Aeschylus, Sophocles and Euripides. Aristophanes wrote comedies which made fun of politicians of the time. Greek playwrights were very busy – not only did they direct their own plays, they also appeared in them.

THE OLYMPIC GAMES

The first Olympic Games were held in the ninth century BC in a small village called Olympia. This was situated in the hills on the west of the Peloponnese, in southern Greece. It is a quiet and peaceful spot. The games started in the following way. Local people believed that the god Zeus visited a grove nearby and they organised sporting competitions in his honour. Soon these games became famous throughout the ancient world, and athletes from all over Greece took part. Foreigners were not allowed to compete, and women were not even allowed to watch. Anyone who broke this ban was guilty of sacrilege and could be put to death.

The Olympic Games were so important to the Greeks that they organised their calendar around them. They took as their starting point the year in which the games were first held, 776 BC. This became the first year of the first Olympiad. So the battle of Marathon, which we say took place in 490 BC, occurred according to the Greeks in the second year of the seventy-second Olympiad.

Between 776 BC and 392 BC the Olympic Games were held every four years. When the games took place, all private quarrels and wars between states were forbidden.

After 392 BC the games were no longer held. Greek civilisation was in decline and athletes found it difficult to train and travel. We know about the history of the early Olympic Games through the work of archaeologists, who in 1875 began to examine the place where the sports were held. Their skilful excavations revealed in great detail what had gone on 2,000 years before.

Pierre de Cubertin organised the first modern Olympic Games in Athens in 1894. He was inspired by what the archaeologists had revealed and wished to revive the Greek ideas of sportsmanship. The games which he started still continue to this day.

The runners' starting line (like the one shown above) was marked by stone slabs with rectangular grooves. The runners could grip these grooves with their toes. The lanes were separated with square wooden posts.

THE OLYMPIC STADIUM

The Olympic track was surrounded by grassy slopes. Crowds of over 20,000 people gathered here to watch the events. The games were so popular and attracted so many competitors that heats and trials were held two months before the official opening.

The Olympic Games lasted a week. The first day was taken up with opening ceremonies. Then came five days of competition, ranging from individual and relay races, to a gruelling race between athletes who wore the full armour of a *hoplite* (illustrated below).

There were also wrestling and boxing matches, and the famous pentathlon, in which young men took part in five events: running, discus, javelin, long jump and wrestling. In the toughest event, the *pancratium*, naked fighters battled, sometimes to the death, using any means they wanted. Only clawing out an opponent's eyes was forbidden!

After the chariot races in the larger hippodrome on the sixth day, there was a final day of feasting and celebration for the victors. The winners received an olive wreath. Back home they were greeted as heroes, and people wrote poems about them.

ALEXANDER THE GREAT

By the fourth century BC, the Greek city-states had become weak because of constant fighting amongst themselves. King Philip II of Macedonia, whose kingdom was in northern Greece, seized this opportunity to gain control of the whole Greek mainland. His ambition was to free the Greek colonies in Asia Minor, who were now ruled by Persia. But he was assassinated before he could put his plan into operation.

Philip's twenty-year-old son, Alexander III, now became king. This remarkable young man was already experienced in the arts of government and warfare. He dreamed of an adventure as exciting as any of the stories in Greek mythology.

You can see how much Alexander conquered by looking at the map opposite. His army of 36,000 foot soldiers and cavalry swept through Asia Minor, Syria, Phoenicia, Egypt (where he founded Alexandria), and Mesopotamia. He created a vast Greek empire. In 326 BC he crossed the River Indus into India. But when he tried to move forward to the River Ganges, his army refused to follow any further into an unknown country, and he was forced to retreat.

From his base in Babylon, Alexander now planned more conquests. His dream was to create a new world, an empire of peace and prosperity. It would combine the best of eastern and western civilisations. But in 323 BC, he suddenly died of malaria, aged only 33. Even today, more than 2,000 years after he died, people still remember Alexander the Great and his extraordinary adventures.

THE BATTLE OF ISSUS

Alexander's most powerful enemy was Darius, King of Persia. The armies of Darius and Alexander met for the last time in 333 BC, near the town of Issus on the northern border of Syria. After ferocious fighting, Darius was forced to flee the field. His army ran away, and Alexander could march straight on to Syria.

THE END OF THE GREEK WORLD

When Alexander the Great lay dying, his most faithful generals gathered about him. They asked him who should be king when he died. 'Whoever is best suited to the task,' he replied. However, after Alexander's death the generals fell out among themselves, and a long period of civil war began. During the fighting Alexander's mother, wife and son, Alexander VI, were all assassinated. Alexander's mighty empire began to break up.

The wars between Alexander's generals continued until 281 BC. A good deal of the fighting was done by mercenaries. There was not too much destruction as the generals wanted to preserve prosperity of the lands they were fighting for. There were many sieges of heavily defended towns, and the attackers developed new kinds of weapons to help them with their assault. One was a huge catapult, eight metres long and five metres high. It could hurl a stone weighing eighty kilograms about 150 metres. Another siege device was a massive tower, covered in metal plates. It was so heavy that it required 3,400 men to move it into position.

When the war finally came to an end, the Greek world was divided into three main kingdoms: Macedonia, under the Antigonid dynasty; Syria, ruled by the Seleucids; and Egypt, under the House of Ptolemy. Athens and Sparta were no longer as powerful as they had been.

After the death of Alexander the Great, a new civilisation sprang up. The original Greek culture is known as Hellenic. The new style was based on the cities founded by Alexander the Great. Many of these were named Alexandria. The new civilisation was called Hellenistic civilisation. It was a combination of Greek culture and the traditions which the Greeks had seen in the east. There was a new emphasis on tolerance. People of different race were accepted, and all types of belief were permitted to mingle together. In this atmosphere creative artists and thinkers flourished. Their work was broader and more individualistic then Hellenic culture. The Hellenistic way of life had a considerable influence on the Roman Empire.

But the age of the Greeks was coming to an end. They came into conflict with the Romans at the end of the third century BC. First the colonies in southern Italy were defeated, then Sicily was captured, and in 168 BC the whole of Greece became a Roman province. Roman armies, led by Pompey the Great, captured Syria and Asia Minor in 64 BC. Cleopatra, Queen of Egypt, committed suicide in 30 BC, and Egypt became part of the mighty Roman Empire. The age of the Romans had begun.

Archimedes lived in the Greek colony of Syracuse in Sicily. He was the most famous scholar of classical times. He made important discoveries in physics and mathematics, and improved the design of catapults. He even designed magnifying glasses which were used to set fire to ships which were attacking his native city.

Some of the finest works of Greek art (like this statue of a fighter) were not produced in Greece itself, but in the Hellenistic cities of Asia Minor. Many beautiful works of art can still be seen today in towns along the coast of Turkey, which was once part of the Greek world. The Romans admired Greek art, and tried to copy it.

For many years the Egyptian city of Alexandria was the centre of learning of the western world. Ctesibius invented several clocks here, and was the first person to think about using compressed air and water as sources of energy. Hero invented a form of steam turbine, shown in the illustration below. The most remarkable discoveries were made in mathematics and astronomy. For example, Hipparchus was the first man to divide a circle into 360°.

ON THE EDGE OF THE GREEK WORLD
THE SCYTHIANS

The Scythians were nomads, who travelled from place to place looking for land and food. They originally came from central Asia, but in about 1,000 BC they began to move south to the shores of the Black Sea and the Caspian Sea. These areas are now all part of the Soviet Union.

This new land was very good for farming. Some Scythians settled down, but others carried on their nomadic lives. They were very good at horse riding and were excellent archers.

Herodotus was a Greek historian who lived in the fifth century BC. He wrote a good deal about the Scythians, so we know how they lived. They travelled and lived in wooden wagons which had four or six wheels. The wagons were covered with felt, and built like small houses. Some had only one room, but the larger ones had three. The wagons were waterproof and also kept out the cold winds. The women and children travelled inside the wagons, and the men followed on horseback, with their herds of cattle and horses. Many Scythians did not stay in one place for long. When there was nothing left for their animals to eat, they moved on.

The Scythians and the Greeks came into contact with each other from about the eighth century BC. Many Greeks went to the shores of the Black Sea, looking for places to fish and for land that could grow wheat. The Scythians bought silver, gold, wine and jewellery from them. Soon they were on very friendly terms with each other. The citizens of Athens even asked a group of Scythian archers to come to their city and help to keep order. These men were the first regular police force in Europe!

When a Scythian chief died, his body was carried about for forty days, followed by members of his tribe. To show their grief they shaved their heads, cut off one ear, and pierced their left hands with arrows. The body was placed in a coffin made of larch wood and decorated with copper figures. Then the dead chief was buried, along with his wives, furniture and jewels.

The wealth of the Scythians came from their cattle and from the animals they hunted. Animal designs were used to decorate buckles, bracelets, vases and even shields. Sometimes a whole animal was shown but often only part of it, like a head or an open jaw. Later, when the Scythians came into contact with the Greeks, they showed humans on their designs as well.

THE CELTS

Celtic civilisation began in central Europe in what is now Czechoslovakia, Austria, Germany and part of Switzerland. In about 700 BC the Celts (whose name comes from the Greek *keltoi*), began to move south and west, and reached the Atlantic, Italy and Spain. Sometimes they came as peaceful settlers, but more often they were aggressive invaders.

By the fourth century BC most Celtic tribes, whom the Romans called *Galli* or Gauls, had settled down in their new lands. But some tribes continued to march into south-east Europe. In 390 BC they attacked Rome. Delphi was burned in 279 BC as they invaded the Adriatic coast, and then Asia Minor. Here they set up the kingdom of Galatia, the land of the Gauls. In time this kingdom passed away, but the name Galatia lasted for many centuries.

The Gauls were a very warlike people, always fighting amongst themselves or with others. Each tribe had a leader, known as a *vergobretus*, elected by a group of leading warriors. The tribe's land was divided between the nobles. Each noble was like a little king, with his own slaves and followers.

The wealthiest Gallic civilisation was in the country that is now France. Like other Gauls, the people of France earned a living by agriculture and trade. This brought them in touch with other Mediterranean civilisations – Greek, Etruscan and Roman. Traders from many Mediterranean lands visited the ports of Provence, in the south, bringing vases, fine cloth and wine. It is interesting that the people living in France had to import wine. Today the French are the most famous wine producers in the world.

Some Gauls worshipped nature gods in woods or by springs. People who were ill would leave a carving of the part of their body which was afflicted near a spring, hoping that the god would cure them. Other Gauls worshipped in single-roomed temples, making gifts and sacrifices to please their gods. Animals were the most frequent offerings, but human sacrifices were also quite common.

Gallic priests were known as Druids. It took twenty years for the Druids to learn by heart the sacred laws and texts. They did not trust the written word. They thought that it could be too easily altered or misunderstood. Other Gauls shared this belief. They wrote very little, and the few written words of theirs which survive are in the Latin or Greek alphabets. The Druids were more powerful than kings or princes. They were not only priests but judges as well.

The Gauls were very good carpenters. Wood was used not only for fuel and house building, but also for making farm implements, carts and ships. The pictures above show how a craftsman made a wooden barrel. Other people in the ancient world marvelled at these barrels.

IRON-CLAD SOLDIERS

Much of the Gauls' success in battle came from the fact that they knew how to make weapons from iron, which was stronger than copper and bronze. It was a very difficult and slow process.

Gallic foot soldiers were armed with iron swords and metal-tipped javelins. For protection they wore helmets, and carried huge shields toughened with metal plates. They also made chain mail from thousands of iron rings, a discovery which the Romans were quick to use for themselves. Only the nobility could afford to keep horses, so they formed the cavalry. When battle began, the Gauls hurled themselves at the enemy in a vast, yelling hoard. Most of their opponents were so terrified by this charge that they turned and fled. But the more disciplined Roman legions stood firm, and drove the Gauls from the field.

A MECHANICAL HARVESTER

The picture on the left shows a mechanical harvester used by the Gauls of northern France. Pliny, a Roman writer, described it, and some carvings have also been found. An ox pushed a 'box' on wheels through the wheat field, and the teeth on its edge tore off ears of wheat, which then fell into the box.

THE ROMANS
THE BIRTH OF ROME

The history of Rome began on the plain of Latium, in what is now Italy, among the fertile hills rising above the left bank of the river Tiber. Shepherds and farmers settled here in the eleventh century BC. They began to grow vines, olives, figs and cereal crops. From their simple huts grew the mighty city of Rome.

The first Romans were farmers and traders. They grew their own food, cut down trees from the surrounding woods to make houses and ships, and sold salt. This was gathered from the lakes at the mouth of the Tiber. Iron and other metals had to be imported from the north.

Seven hills surrounded ancient Rome. The Palatine hill was the first to be inhabited, followed by settlements on the Esquiline and Quirinal hills. By about 650 BC these small villages began to form a town, with brick houses, streets, and a wooden bridge over the Tiber. At the centre, between the Palatine and Caelian hills, lay a broad square, known as the Forum.

Roman craftsmen became famous as metal workers. Trade grew, and people learned to write. The merchants, farmers, manufacturers and slaves were controlled by a handful of rich and powerful families. At the time the use of writing became more widespread. This helped culture to develop. Trade and manufacture blossomed. Rome was fortunate in being well-placed for communication wth the Greeks, Phoenicians and Etruscans.

For over one hundred years Rome was ruled by Etruscan kings. They built a huge palace and a temple to Jupiter on the Capitoline hill. King Servius Tullius built a huge defensive stone wall round the entire city. Finally, in 509 BC, the Romans rebelled against their Etruscan masters. Tarquin the Proud, the last Etruscan king, was thrown out of the city, and Rome became a republic.

A famous legend is told about the founding of Rome. It is best related by the poet Virgil in his poem the *Aeneid*. He said that after Troy was captured, Aeneas, a Trojan noble, fled to Italy. His son, Ascanius, founded the city of Alba there. Many centuries later two descendants of the Kings of Alba, baby twins called Romulus and Remus, were abandoned in their cradle on the river Tiber.

The boys were miraculously kept alive by a she-wolf, and then rescued by a shepherd. When they grew up they founded a city on the Palatine hill. But the brothers quarrelled. Remus was killed, and Romulus became king of the city. This city took its name from him: Rome.

This famous statue of Romulus and Remus being suckled by a she-wolf was begun in the fifth century BC. The figures of the twin boys were added hundreds of years later.

At first the Romans burned their dead bodies, keeping the ashes in little house-shaped urns, like the one shown here. However, in the seventh century BC they began burying their dead, like the Greeks and the Etruscans.

This picture shows an early Roman village. Later the city spread over seven hills, the Palatine, Esquiline, Caelian, Viminal, Quirinal, Capitoline and Aventine. A massive stone wall encircled the whole city.

THE GROWTH OF THE REPUBLIC

After the Etruscan kings had been driven out, Rome was governed by a Senate of 300 members, and two consuls. The consuls had power for only a year. This was to prevent them becoming like the old tyrannical kings. Only members of the wealthy nobility – the patricians – could become consuls or senators. The patricians also owned most of the good farmland. The ordinary people, known as plebeians, had no say in the government. They had to serve in the army and work in lowly jobs. This made them very dissatisfied, so that at one time they threatened to found a new city of their own. Gradually, however, the plebeians improved their lot. In 494 BC Rome's laws were published, so that everyone knew their rights. Later plebeians were allowed to become senators and consuls. The new emblem of Rome became SPQR. It stood for the Senate and People of Rome.

The Romans were very powerful because of their wealth and their strong armies. Unlike many of their enemies they were also proud of their city. This patriotism gave them additional strength. They set about conquering the whole of the Italian peninsula. Etruria was the fist state they captured. Then they overcame the Greek colonies in southern Italy and on Sicily. They defeated Carthage in the lengthy Punic wars. By the first century AD, Rome controlled every country around the Mediterranean. The great landlocked sea had almost become a Roman lake. Defeats by the Gauls and Hannibal had now become just bad memories.

Corinth, whose ruins are shown above, was captured by the Romans in 146 BC.

The Romans' ships were built with huge decks for their well-trained soldiers to fight on. The navy first attacked with archers, and rams fitted to the bows of their ships. Then they lowered gangways, with massive spikes at the end, on to the enemy boats. Legionaries charged over these temporary bridges and slaughtered the enemy before they had time to organise themselves. The most famous victory using these tactics was against the Carthaginians, off Mylae in 260 BC.

ROMAN GODS

The Romans adopted many of the Greeks' gods, and changed their names. Zeus became Jupiter, Hera was known as Juno, and Athena and Dionysus were called Minerva and Bacchus. The Romans built their temples in the Greek style, with tall columns on the outside. They also had household gods, who looked after the *domus* or home.

Julius Caesar (101-44 BC)

Julius Caesar was born into an ancient Roman family. He was an ambitious, well-educated and intelligent man, who became consul in 59 BC. He had many powerful supporters in Rome. The next year, at the age of forty-two, he began the conquest of Gaul. In 55 BC he even made an expedition into southern Britain.

Caesar was now a true hero of the Roman people and made many other conquests. One of Caesar's famous sayings was, 'Veni, vidi, vici', which means, 'I came, I saw, I conquered'. In 45 BC he returned to Rome in triumph. He made many changes in the government of Rome, established new colonies, and set up a new calendar, which we still use today.

But Caesar was becoming too powerful. People began to worship him as a god, and he allowed the month of Julius to be named after him. This is where the word July comes from. His enemies plotted against him. In the end, Caesar was assassinated by a group of senators on the Ides of March (March 15) in 44 BC.

THE AGE OF AUGUSTUS

Julius Caesar had an adopted son, Octavian. After Caesar's death there was a struggle for power between Octavian and Mark Antony, which Octavian had won by 29 BC. He had great authority: he was commander-in-chief of the army (*imperator*), guardian of Roman religion, and he had the right to overrule the Senate's decisions. But he did not try to make himself king. He upheld the laws of the Republic, and did not interfere with the Senate's discussions or the work of the magistrates.

After many years of civil war Octavian brought peace to Rome. He conquered new territories, the government was reorganised, and the Republic's finances were straightened out. In 27 BC he was given the title of Augustus (which means 'Venerable' or 'Respected'). This title had been used before only for holy places. By 2 BC Augustus was known as Father of the Republic. He was the most powerful man in the western world.

When Augustus died in 14 AD the Romans hailed him as a god. Temples and shrines were built in his honour. Augustus had chosen Tiberius to be the next leader. He was accepted and automatically became emperor. The Republic had gone and Rome had now become an empire that was to last for 400 years.

At first Tiberius ruled well, but later he became a tyrant. His successors, Caligula, Claudius and Nero, also showed great cruelty. After the wise governments of Vespasian and Titus, the empire once more suffered under tyrannical rule. Domitian's behaviour was as bad as that of any of the previous tyrants. But the day-to-day administration did not suffer. This time of peace, known as the *Pax Romana* or peace of Rome, carried on all over the Mediterranean world.

All this time the reputation of Augustus grew. Many stories were told about him, and the Romans believed that his life had been protected by the gods. He became the leading hero of the empire. The historian Suetonius wrote a remarkable description of him:

> 'He was very handsome, with a calm and unruffled appearance. Anyone who gazed into his clear eyes soon had to look away, for they shone with the brightness of the sun.'

Octavian, who was later known as Augustus, was the first Roman emperor. He was the great-nephew of Julius Caesar and fought with him in Spain. He gained complete control over the Roman Republic sixteen years after Caesar's death. When Augustus died, Tiberius took over, and the Republic became an empire.

The Romans were the first to build triumphal arches to celebrate their victories. The one shown here is in Thuburbo Majus, Tunisia. In modern times similar arches were built in London (Marble Arch) and Paris (the Arc de Triomphe).

By the time of Julius Caesar the Romans held great victory parades whenever they made new conquests. The processions wound their way from the Field of Mars, through the *Forum*, then up to the Capitol hill. First came the senators and magistrates. Then came the trumpeters and a display of captured articles, all carefully labelled. Then captives were brought out in chains, and behind them came the victorious general himself, riding in a chariot. Wearing a crown of laurel leaves, he was dressed like Jupiter, the king of the gods.

THE EMPIRE AT ITS HEIGHT

The Roman Empire was at its most powerful in the second century AD. It stretched from the sands of the Sahara to the Scottish border, and from the Black Sea to the Atlantic.

The empire covered an area far larger than the present European Community, and it had a population of many tens of millions. It was divided into forty-three provinces so that it could be governed efficiently. Each one had its own governor.

Fine towns were built in stone and marble all over the empire. Usually these were laid out in a grid pattern, with straight roads crossing each other at right angles. The principal roads were known as the *cardo* and the *decumanus*. The main square, or *forum*, was placed where the main north-south and east-west roads crossed. Around it clustered all the most important buildings: temples, law courts, business centres and government offices. The larger cities also took pride in putting up fine public buildings, such as baths, theatres, amphitheatres and race tracks.

Goods poured into Ostia, the port of Rome, from every corner of the empire. Wheat, wine and oil came from Gaul and the North African coast. Britain, Spain and the Danube basin provided tin, iron, copper and silver. Wild animals were imported for the cruel entertainment of the people. The east provided the luxury goods demanded by the wealthy, such as silks and jewellery.

The empire was so rich from the taxes which it raised from trade that it could afford to hand out free food to the citizens of Rome. This took the form of grain, fruit, vegetables and even meat. The empire's income came principally from customs duties, sales taxes and large sums of money sent to Rome from the provinces.

Roman citizenship could be granted to subjects from any part of the empire. This was a sort of passport, which gave them special protection and privileges wherever they were. All citizens could attend the Senate at Rome.

Emperor Trajan (53-117 AD) was not born in Italy, but in Spain. He conquered more land in Asia. Hadrian (117-138 AD), Trajan's adopted son and successor, travelled widely throughout the empire. Antonius Pius, emperor from 138 to 161 AD governed without leaving Rome. Marcus Aurelius (161-180 AD), a philosopher and statesman, was the last emperor to govern the empire while it was at its most powerful. He had to deal with Germanic tribes in the Danube area who were threatening to invade. His death from plague, while campaigning against the invaders, marked the end of Rome's greatest period.

Hadrian's Wall runs across northern England, from the Tyne to the Solway. It was built between 122 and 126 AD by the emperor Hadrian, to protect the northern frontier of his empire. There were small forts, like the one shown here, every mile of its length. Much of the wall can still be seen today.

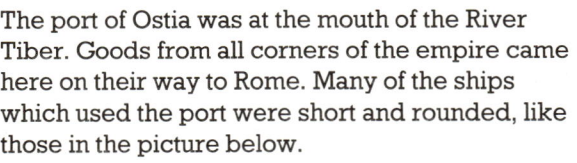

The port of Ostia was at the mouth of the River Tiber. Goods from all corners of the empire came here on their way to Rome. Many of the ships which used the port were short and rounded, like those in the picture below.

The temple on the right was built in the second century AD at Baalbek in Lebanon. The columns are 19 m tall, and the whole impressive building was dedicated to Bacchus.

The Romans allowed conquered people to keep their own religions, as long as they included the emperor as one of their gods. This custom helped to hold the empire together.

THE BEST SOLDIERS IN THE WORLD

For hundreds of years the Roman army was probably the best in the world. Its strength was the main reason why the Roman Empire grew so large. The army was made up of people of all classes. The rich citizens joined the cavalry, those less well-off made up the heavy infantry. Each soldier was well armoured, wearing a breastplate, helmet and leg guards (known as greaves). He carried a sword, a spear and a solid shield. The poorest people were lightly armed with slings.

The army developed new tactics after it was defeated by the Gauls in 390 BC. The two front lines of soldiers advanced first, armed with javelins. They hurled these at the enemy from close range, then attacked with their short stabbing swords. Behind them was a third line of soldiers who carried lances. The infantry (foot soldiers) wore metal armour and carried heavy rectangular shields.

General Marius organised the army in a more professional way at the end of the second century BC. Infantrymen joined up for sixteen years, and the cavalry for ten. Veterans, who had completed their service, were rewarded with grants of land. The army was divided into legions of 6,000 men. The chief fighting unit was called a century of one hundred soldiers, commanded by a centurion. Each legion was capable of fighting on its own, for it had its own administration, health corps and engineers.

The Roman army developed successful tactics to prevent surprise attacks by the enemy. A marching column of soldiers was defended by scouts and outriders. When it stopped for the night, some troops built an armed camp, surrounded with a ditch and an earth wall, others searched for food, and a third group stood guard.

Roman soldiers were known as legionaries. They had to be completely self-sufficient, carrying on their backs everything they needed for a campaign. This included not only weapons, but tools, bedding and cooking utensils.

FORTIFIED CAMPS

The Romans were very skilled at building fortified bases for their legions. The most famous was constructed by Julius Caesar's army at Alesia in Gaul, shown in the picture above. His men built two huge earth ramparts around the large hill which they were defending. They protected these banks of earth with ditches, wooden walls and towers, and a series of cunning traps.

The Romans tried several different designs of military helmet. The one shown here is known as the 'jockey cap' because of its long peak at the front. It gave plenty of protection but must have been very hot to wear.

This catapult was used to attack enemy camps. It could throw a stone weighing 60 kg about 200 m.

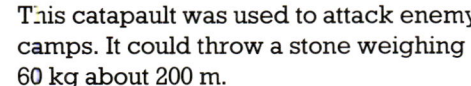

The secrets of the Romans' success in battles were attention to detail and very strict discipline. Each soldier was well-armed and well looked after. But the punishments were ferocious for a man who disobeyed orders. Cowardice in battle was the most serious offence. Men guilty of this were beaten or stoned to death.

LIFE IN ROME

Rome was the largest city in the classical world. Many of its 2 million inhabitants lived in hastily built blocks of flats. The Emperor Trajan ordered that these were not to be more than eighteen metres high, but they were still very dangerous. Sometimes they collapsed, and in the dry summer months fires often swept through them. The palaces of the emperors and expensive villas of the rich were much safer.

People, goods and religions from all over the empire could be found in Rome. It was possible to stand in the Forum and hear spoken not only the Latin of the Romans, but also the languages of Britain, Arabia, Germany, Gaul and a host of other Roman provinces. Rome really did seem to be the centre of the world. People flocked there from all the corners of the empire. They expected to find wealth. They grew restless if their wishes were not met.

Preserving order in Rome was not easy. The authorities kept the population happy with gifts of free food, and by providing non-stop entertainment. Almost 250,000 people crowded into the Circus Maximus (a large stadium) for thrilling chariot races. Sometimes there were a hundred races a day. Just as popular were games held in the Colosseum, another huge stadium, built in the first century BC. In the first hundred days after it was opened, 9,000 animals and 2,000 gladiators died in fights, watched by bloodthirsty crowds.

WATER SUPPLY

Rome needed enormous amounts of water – 1,000,000 m³ a day. This is almost double the amount supplied to modern cities which are the same size as ancient Rome. Eleven stone aqueducts (water bridges), like the one shown above, carried the water from rivers and springs into the city. It was then filtered and distributed through underground lead pipes to the city's thousands of fountains, baths and troughs.

The picture below shows the Forum, the great square which lay in the centre of Rome. It was built by the last Etruscan kings on a flat drained area between three of the city's hills. All around it stood temples and important public buildings, such as the *curia*, where the Senate met. Here too was the House of the Vestals, who were responsible for guarding Rome's sacred fire. At one end of the Forum there were platforms where politicians could address the crowds. There was also a Golden Milestone, which had carved on it the distances between Rome and the major cities of the empire. Traders set up their stalls here early in the morning.

POMPEII

In 79 AD Mount Vesuvius suddenly erupted. The small city of Pompeii, which lay in the volcano's shadow, was completely buried in ash and lava. Archaeologists have now excavated the site, uncovering unique evidence of what daily life in a Roman city was like.

Pompeii had a population of about 15,000 inhabitants. It lay at the centre of rich farmlands. A small group of wealthy bankers, landowners, businessmen and merchants governed the city. They were very proud of it and paid for fine public buildings, such as baths and an amphitheatre. The rest of the population, both slaves and free men, were poor but they earned enough for all their basic needs such as food and housing.

The large houses of the wealthy were built around courtyards. In these shady gardens, with their flowers and fountains, the rich could escape from the noise and heat of the streets. Shopkeepers lived above their businesses, and other citizens rented rooms in blocks of flats.

The busy streets were the heart of city life, lined with shops and inns. Here people did their shopping or just gossiped on the pavement. Taverns served tasty snacks of soup and vegetables for those who felt hungry between meals. Wine was the most popular drink. It was often watered down so that people who drank too much did not get tipsy. Only in the evening, when people went in for their main meal (the *cena*), did the streets become quiet again.

THE STREET OF PLENTY

The picture above is of one of Pompeii's main streets. Archaeologists have named it the 'street of plenty' because of the large number of businesses found there. Most buildings were shops, with counters opening directly on to the street. Almost every kind of business could be found here, from lampmakers to laundries.

Just like a modern city, the walls of Pompeii were covered in graffiti. On one wall an innkeeper recorded the date when he bottled his olives. On another, a drinker boasted of his adventures with a serving girl.

When Vesuvius erupted on 24 August, 79 AD, many of Pompeii's inhabitants were quickly covered in lava. The lava hardened over the bodies, which rotted away, leaving hollows. By pouring plaster into these hollows, scientists have been able to reproduce figures just as they were when they died.

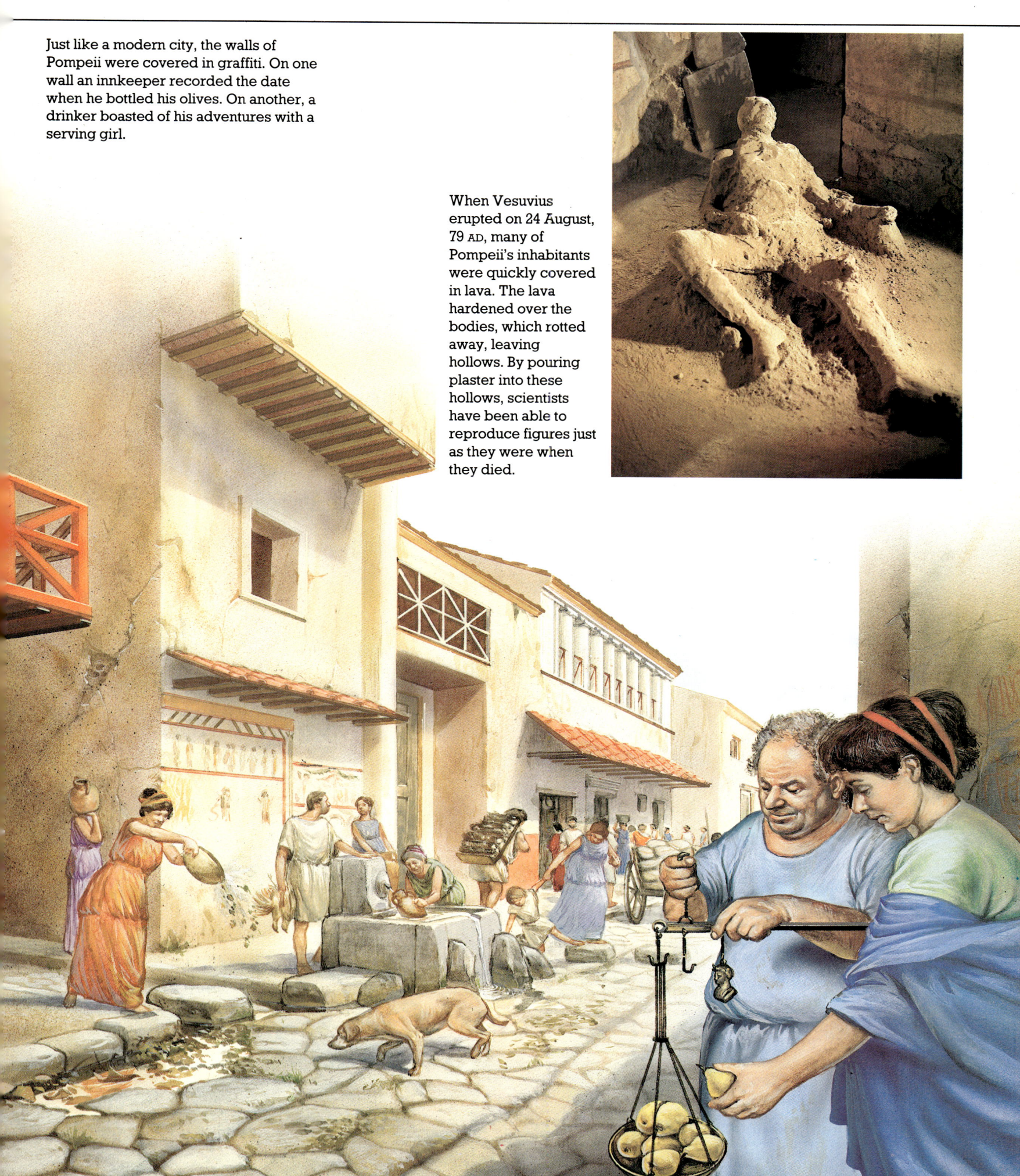

THE REMAINS OF THE EMPIRE

The remains of the Roman Empire can be found all over the classical world. There are walls, mosaics and columns in areas as far apart as Scotland and Morocco, Portugal and Syria. Archaeologists can use these remains to build up a complete picture of life in Roman times. In many places the way people lived did not change very much, just because they were governed by Rome.

Strong civilisations were not much altered by the arrival of the Romans. In some cases they influenced the Romans more than the Romans influenced them. The Greeks were part of the Roman Empire for many centuries. Nevertheless, they continued to build temples, such as those at Caria and Lycia, in their traditional style. The Egyptians also kept their own style of architecture for the famous Nile temples. In other areas local languages and customs continued unchanged, especially in Asia Minor where Greek was still widely spoken.

Roman influence was strongest in areas where the original civilisation had not been very well developed. This was particularly the case in England, Gaul, Spain and North Africa. It is not very easy to discover how people lived in these countries before the Roman legions arrived.

But the Romans brought many benefits when they conquered a country. They introduced education, a system of law and new entertainments, all of which changed people's lives.

The Romans were magnificent road builders. Thousands of kilometres of fine highway ran to every corner of the empire. These long straight roads meant that the legions could travel swiftly to trouble spots, and traders could move their goods with ease. Several modern English roads, such as the Watling Street (A5), follow the routes first chosen by Roman engineers. They are as straight as motorways. Nothing stood in the way of a Roman road. It was carried across valleys on viaducts and tunnelled through mountains. Using these roads, the Emperor Augustus created an efficient mail service. Special carriages could carry letters all over the empire at a rate of 75 km a day.

THE ROMAN GAMES

Almost all cities in the empire built stadiums, like the one above, for races, fights and other bloodthirsty entertainments. Sometimes men and women had to battle for their lives with starving lions. There were always contests between gladiators, who fought each other to the death with swords, nets and spears.

This stone is carved with a decree in Latin issued by the Emperor Vespasian. Stones like this, known as *stelae*, were set up in public places so that people could read the government's laws and orders. Greek was the language of scholars, but Latin was the official language of the Roman Empire. It was used for all laws and official letters. Latin was also used by famous historians, such as Livy and Tacitus, and poets like Virgil and Horace.

This wall at Jublains in France shows the Roman technique of building. The Romans used stones and bricks in layers, and so put up very solid walls which have lasted for centuries.

63

THE FALL OF ROME

The Roman Empire was large and difficult to manage. It could be threatened by enemies outside, or by internal disagreements. In the third century AD some provinces began to break away from the empire and declare themselves independent. Trier on the river Rhine became the capital of a separate Gallic empire. In the east the city of Palmyra also broke away from Rome. Much of the trouble came from generals who used their soldiers to fight against other sections of their own army.

Law and order began to break down. Pirates attacked merchant ships on the Mediterranean, famines swept the land, and money began to lose its value. Most dangerous of all were the attacks of Germanic tribes from the north and east.

The Emperor Aurelian, who came to power in 270, managed to keep things calm for a while. But invasion was still a serious threat, and defensive walls were built around Rome and other cities. Diocletian (245-313), became emperor at the end of the third century, and tried dividing power between four joint emperors (tetrarchs). But the experiment failed and Diocletian retired to a splendid palace in his native land of Dalmatia.

After a period of civil war Constantine became emperor. He had been one of the tetrarchs. He is remembered for two reforms. He recognised Christianity as an official religion. Before this the Christians had been persecuted in horrible ways throughout the empire. He also transferred his capital from Rome to Byzantium in what is now Turkey. The city's name was changed to Constantinople.

After Constantine's death in 338 there was squabbling and fighting throughout the empire. Emperor Theodosius managed to unite it for one last time in 379. He did so by using barbarians in the Roman army. The trouble was that these new soldiers did not have the same loyal attitude towards the empire as Roman citizens did. When he died in 395, the empire was split between his sons, Arcadius and Honorius. Arcadius set up an empire in Constantinople which lasted for another thousand years, but Honorius' empire, centred on Milan, soon collapsed. It was overcome by tribes from Germany and other areas beyond the empire's northern frontier.

Rome was attacked by a tribe called the Visigoths in 410. Wave after wave of attackers then continued to sweep through the western empire, until the last emperor was removed from power in 476. His name combined that of Rome's founder and the first emperor: Romulus Augustulus. The Roman Empire had ceased to exist.

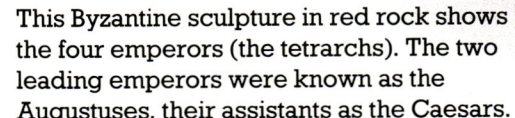

This Byzantine sculpture in red rock shows the four emperors (the tetrarchs). The two leading emperors were known as the Augustuses, their assistants as the Caesars.

The Romans called all those who lived outside the empire 'barbarians'. The most ferocious were the Huns, led by Attila, from central Asia. Other leading tribes were the Franks, who settled in northern France, the Burgundians who carved out a kingdom for themselves along the River Rhone, and the Visigoths who conquered Spain and southern France. The destructive Vandals reached several Mediterranean islands and North Africa. Much of Italy was captured by the Ostrogoths. England was overwhelmed by Angles, Saxons and Jutes from northern Germany. This movement of people from one area to another caused huge political and social changes in Europe.

THE ARRIVAL OF CHRISTIANITY

Roman religion was very formal, concerned more with ceremonies than with belief. The religions of the east were more interested in spiritual matters. Some had very strange ceremonies. A follower of the Persian sun-God, Mithras, would lie in a pit while above him a bull had its throat cut. The warm blood then sprinkled all over him.

Christianity began in the east, among the Jews of Judea. To many of them Jesus Christ was the saviour (or Messiah). They believed that Jesus rose from the dead after he had been crucified by the Romans. His followers, who called themselves Christians, travelled widely around the Mediterranean. They spread the good news (gospel) that God's son had visited earth to free people from sin and give them a chance of eternal life. They taught people to love their neighbours and obey the commandments of the one God.

At first Christians were badly treated for refusing to worship the emperor. But the faith continued to grow and organise itself. The bishop of Rome became its leader, or pope. Finally, the Emperor Constantine was converted to Christianity on his death bed. The religion which had started from such humble beginnings three centuries previously was now the main religion of the empire.

BYZANTIUM

Byzantine civilisation, which grew up in Byzantium was much more than just an offshoot of Rome. After all, it survived for 1,123 years (300-1453), far longer than the Roman Empire.

The city of Byzantium was founded in about 660 BC as a Greek colony. About 1,000 years later Constantine made it the capital of the Roman Empire, and changed its name to Constantinople. It lay at the entrance to the Black Sea, between Asia and Europe – an ideal position for keeping control of the eastern Mediterranean. They were not able to recapture the land which the invaders had seized in the west. But the Emperor Justinian and his general, Belisarius, did manage to seize most of the territory around the Adriatic.

Like Rome, Constantinople contained many magnificent public buildings. There were gorgeous palaces, public baths, a broad forum, and a stadium – the hippodrome – which held 100,000 spectators. Also, being a Christian city, it had hundreds of churches. The most impressive of these was St Sophia. Emperor Justinian began building it in 532. This splendid church was one of the wonders of the eastern Mediterranean.

In 381 the leader of the Byzantine Church claimed that he had equal power with the pope in Rome. Before long the Roman Catholic Church had become completely separated from the Orthodox Church (the name given to the Byzantine Church). Hundreds of new Christian churches were built throughout Byzantium.

Constantinople rivalled Rome in leisure activities, too. Although its inhabitants didn't go in for the sort of bloodthirsty games which had so delighted the Romans, they had four theatres. These put on shows during 101 of the city's 179 public holidays. Chariot racing was the most popular sport. A well-known Byzantine motto was: 'St Sophia is God's; the palace is the emperor's; but the hippodrome belongs to the people.'

Byzantine civilisation influenced the whole of Europe and the Middle East. Much of the art and architecture of Islam was based on examples found in Byzantium. The religion, writing and culture of eastern Europe came from Byzantium. Also, for many year scholars from western Europe had to rely on Byzantium to find out about the classical world of Greece and Rome.

Although they were Christians, the Byzantine emperors lived in much the same way as the old Roman emperors had done. They enjoyed great luxury, and were almost regarded as gods. They had two thrones in their palace, one for themselves and a second, always empty, for Christ. Emperors were chosen by the Senate, army and people. Any clever and ambitious person could try to become emperor, however poor his background. Leo I had previously been a butcher, and Michael III was a servant. Basil I was the most remarkable of all: he had been a slave.

It took 10,000 labourers, working for 5 years (532-537), to complete the church of St Sophia. Gold, silver, ivory and marble were used to build it. When it was finished the Emperor Justinian thanked God for allowing him to build a temple more magnificent than that of King Solomon. Today the domed building is a mosque, for Constantinople was captured by the Muslim Turks in 1453. Nowadays Constantinople is known as Istanbul.

RESEARCHING THE PAST

Illustrations like this one of a mother looking after her young child were rare by the second century AD. Small families were the most common and a mother of more than two children was widely honoured.

FAMILY LIFE IN CLASSICAL TIMES

The ancient Greeks and Romans did not like having large families. Children were expensive to keep, and when the father died, the family wealth would have to be divided between them all. There was no means of birth control, and unwanted babies were left to die. The father decided which children to keep. Romans had eight days to make up their minds with baby girls, and nine with boys. Unwanted Greek babies were left on the temple steps, but in Rome they were simply abandoned on the local rubbish tip.

There are plenty of examples of babies being rescued from these dreadful places, but this was not usually done out of kindness. The rescuers wanted to bring up the children themselves, then use them as slaves in their households or on their estates. Only occasionally were babies rescued by people who wished to give them a decent life.

Since men in those days were considered more important than women, it was usually female babies who were left to die. Only when Christianity became the official religion of the Roman Empire was this killing of babies abolished.

Children's names

In Athens, once a father had decided to keep a son, the baby was paraded around the family altar in the arms of his parents. Then he was officially named at a banquet to which members of the family and close friends were invited. He was given three names: a first name, his father's name, and the name of the district where he was born. At a Roman naming ceremony the baby boy was sprinkled with water, and a locket containing lucky charms was hung round his neck.

Like the Greeks, the Romans also gave their boys three names. The first (*praenomen*) was the name of one of the distant ancestors from whom the family was descended. Then came the *nomen*, or family name. This was followed by the *cognomen* which showed the difference between branches of the same family. Caesar's full name was Gaius Julius Caesar.

In both Greece and Rome girls were given only one name, such as Livia or Cornelia, female versions of the family name.

This Roman copy of a Greek bronze statue probably represents Pericles' beautiful mistress, Aspasia.

Divorce was rare when Rome was a Republic, but increased considerably when it became an Empire. At first only men were allowed to start a divorce, but gradually women also could do this.

A woman's world

In both Greece and Rome, women were regarded as second-class citizens. They were not allowed to play any part in politics. Girls had to obey their fathers, and wives were completely under their husbands' control. Even widows had to do what their sons told them. If a married woman had no son, her husband appointed a guardian to look after her in the event of his death. The houses of the wealthy had special quarters set aside for the women. This was known in Greek as the *gynaeceum*.

Only occasionally were women allowed to go out to attend festivals or family ceremonies. They were never allowed out on their own. Strangely, women did not have to be kept in by bolts and bars. They were afraid to go out without an escort. If they were seen in the streets alone then the whole family was disgraced. This meant a severe punishment for the woman.

Women in ancient Greece and Rome did not choose their husbands. A husband was picked for them by their parents. The engagement ceremony was an important occasion, when sacrifices were made to the household gods, and the man gave his fiancée a ring for her left hand. This custom has lasted for hundreds of years, and is still followed today in many parts of the world. The reason why the second finger of the left hand was chosen is explained by the Roman writer, Aulus Gellius. He said 'when human corpses are cut open a thin nerve can be found running directly from the heart to the ring finger.' The Egyptians, who were better scientists then the Romans, discovered this interesting fact. Even in those days the heart was believed to be the part of the body controlling love.

Influential women

One group of women in ancient Greece had much more freedom than most others. These were the prostitutes and mistresses of the wealthy. Usually they were not Greek citizens but slaves or free foreigners. They were not kept cooped up in the *gynaeceum*, but were free to attend male parties and discussion groups. They learned about philosophy, and the art of writing and speaking poetry. In this way some of them became well educated. Pericles, a Greek politician, was so fond of his mistress, Aspasia, that he even allowed her to break the laws which he had made himself. She was one of the most intelligent and cultivated women in ancient Greece.

Only in Sparta were boys and girls treated exactly the same. The girls were trained to be fit, strong and brave, ready to be mothers of the next generation of soldiers. The Spartans believed that healthy mothers would produce sons who would make capable soldiers.

Life for women improved in Rome over the years. Some were put in charge of running large households, and wives (who were known as *Matronae*) were allowed to sit beside their husbands at meal times. Husbands often sought their wives' advice on important matters. This custom came from the Etruscans, the people of northern Italy who had allowed women to live reasonably normal lives. This meant that women had a good deal of influence behind the scenes. Some emperors' wives were very powerful, such as Livia, who married Augustus, and Trajan's wife, Plotina. These women helped to make decisions which affected the whole empire.

RESEARCHING THE PAST

THE TRAVELS OF ULYSSES

Very few writings by Greek authors have survived. They wrote by hand on scrolls made from papyrus reeds. The work was then copied and recopied over the years. Sometimes a scribe made a mistake. This was then copied. Eventually there was no way of telling what the author had originally said. What was popular one year was not always so well liked the next. There were only a few writings which were thought to be worth saving by every civilisation. Tastes changed. New religions came along, demanding that old customs be forgotten. In this way most plays, poems and other pieces of writing were censored, destroyed or simply ignored. There were 150 writers of tragedy in ancient Greece, but the plays of only three of them have survived until today. These writers are Aeschylus, Sophocles and Euripides. We know that between them they wrote over 300 plays, but only thirty-three are left.

Ulysses' voyage

For seven years Ulysses lived with a nymph named Calypso on the island of Ogygia. This may have been based on a real peninsula near Gibraltar.

On the island of Aeaea a sorceress called Circe turned Ulysses' friends into pigs, but Ulysses himself escaped because he had eaten a magic plant.

Ulysses met the one-eyed giant, Polythemus, on an island which could have been present-day Sicily.

For seven years Ulysses lived with a nymph named Calypso on the island of Ogygia. This may have been based on a real peninsula near Gibraltar.

The island of Ithaca, where Ulysses finally finished his legendary journey.

Off southern Italy Ulysses survived clashing rocks, a whirlpool, and the enticements of beautiful girls who tried to shipwreck sailors.

Homer described the land of the lotus-eaters, where those who ate a delicious fruit forgot their past lives. This may have been an island off North Africa.

Homer

Homer is one of the most famous Greek writers. His two long poems, the *Iliad* and the *Odyssey*, have lasted to this day with few cuts or changes. Homer was so popular that the Greeks called him simply 'the poet'. His works were as well-known in the ancient world as the Bible was in Christian Europe. No library in the ancient world was complete without an edition of Homer's works. This popularity continued into the Middle Ages and to the time of the Renaissance. Homer's stories are still read today, and feature films have been made of them. Some fragments of papyrus were found recently in Egypt, and more than half of them contained extracts from Homer's poems.

We do not know much about Homer, but he was born in the eighth century BC, probably on the island of Chios off the mainland of Greece. He died on the island of Los. He belonged to a group of wandering poets who chanted their poems to music which they played on the lyre. These men wandered from town to town, entertaining the rich in their houses and the kings in their palaces. However, Homer did something new. Using the recently invented Greek alphabet, he wrote down the *Iliad* and the *Odyssey*, so everyone could read them.

These two great poems are based on the legends of Mycenaean civilisation, and the war between Greeks and Trojans. Homer learned the stories of these people from tales which were handed down from generation to generation, not in writing, but using the spoken word. He told what had happened long ago and he also put in descriptions of his own world. The armour he described has been checked with the discoveries of archaeologists: the poet was correct in every detail. He also knew all about the coasts of the eastern Mediterranean, from Italy to Egypt. But he was less sure about the west. Like all Greeks, he believed that the world was a giant saucer, whose edge lay somewhere west of Gibraltar. If sailors ventured too far in this direction they could fall off the edge of the world!

Troy, which Ulysses left on his ten-year voyage home after it had been captured by the Greeks.

Over the centuries, hundreds of scholars have tried to piece together Homer's descriptions of the places visited by Ulysses. It is impossible to work out exactly where he went, but this map is based on the most reasonable suggestions. Ulysses set out to sail from Troy to Ithaca, his home. The journey should have taken only a few weeks, but because of all the disasters on the way, he didn't reach home until ten years later.

The excavation of Troy

The man who first discovered the site of Troy was Heinrich Schliemann, the son of a German priest. When he was a child he was fascinated by stories of the ancient world. But his parents were too poor to keep him at school, so he began work in a grocer's shop.

Six years later he worked as a cabin boy on a ship and over the next few years had many adventures, including being shipwrecked. He also learned several foreign languages, and used his skills to make a fortune in trade with Russia. At last in 1866, at the age of forty-four, he was free to retire from business and work as a full-time archaeologist.

In 1870 Schliemann and his young Greek wife, Sophie, began excavations at Hissarlik in modern-day Turkey where he believed Troy had once stood. At the time scholars did not know for certain where Troy had stood. Some believed that the city had been further south, near Bunarbashi. After three years, assisted by over a hundred labourers, he had uncovered many remains of the ancient city. His most exciting discovery came right at the end of the dig, on 15 June 1873. He noticed something gleaming at the bottom of a deep pit. He sent the workers away on holiday, then began digging. To their amazement he and his wife uncovered a wonderful hoard of jewels. Schliemann thought he had found the treasure of King Priam, but in fact the jewels were much older. He gave the treasure to the museum of Berlin, where it was displayed. But during the second World War, it disappeared, and has never been seen since.

This Roman mosaic shows sea nymphs, called sirens. They tried to tempt Ulysses and his companions towards the shore, so that they would be shipwrecked on the hidden rocks.

RESEARCHING THE PAST

DIVING INTO THE PAST

In the second century BC a Roman ship left the island of Delos, off the Greek mainland. She was heading into the sunset for the western Mediterranean. She might have been going to Spain, or even out of the Mediterranean altogether. Near Naples the sailors took on some varnished pottery, and then set sail again. She was making for Massilia.

But the richly laden ship never arrived. We do not know exactly what happened to her – perhaps she ran into a storm or hit a reef – but she sank in sixty metres of water off the coast of southern Gaul (present-day France). The exact point where she went down was at the eastern tip of the Isle de Riou. All the crew drowned.

The evidence of the jars

Two thousand years later the wreck was discovered by the French diver, Jacques Cousteau. He was working with a group of scientists and archaeologists from a special ship, the *Calypso*. Between 1952 and 1961, over 400 storage jars (*amphorae*) and thousands of pieces of pottery were brought up from the sea bed. They were closely examined to find out what they had contained, where they came from, and where they were being taken. This was the beginning of modern underwater archaeology.

In the first half of the twentieth century wrecks were explored in search of valuable works of art. The men who did this were more like pirates than scientists. In 1907 a wreck containing valuable bronzes and marbles was discovered off the Tunisian coast, near Mahdia. Over the next six years all the wreck's works of art were brought to the surface and sold to dealers. Today divers are much more scientific. Underwater archaeologists first photograph and measure the wreck they are examining, before bringing up everything they can to the surface. Because of underwater archaeology we have been able to learn a great deal about early Mediterranean civilisations and how they traded with each other. Wrecks in deep water, lying in mud or silt, have survived over hundreds of years. On the other hand, ships that sank in shallow water are much less well preserved. Unlike silt, sand and weed do not protect wood from rotting. A ship's hull and superstructure soon disintegrate if they are not protected.

Traders in ancient times labelled their *amphorae* very carefully. This was rather like a tin of food which we buy from the supermarket, with information on its contents clearly printed on the outside. On each jar was the seal of the potter who made it, its weight when both full and empty, the name of the merchant, the area where the contents came from, and often the address where the jar was going. Historians can learn a lot from this valuable information.

The wrecks themselves teach us a lot about how ships were made. When a ship carrying a heavy cargo sank, the goods fell to the bottom of the hold. Slowly they were covered in silt, so the outline of the ship's hull was preserved for ever in the mud. There were three main types of cargo ship in Roman times. They ranged from fifteen to forty metres long. The largest ones carried 5,000 *amphorae*. It would have needed hundreds of ox carts to carry such a load on land. The Romans even had a sort of wine tanker, with enormous jars two metres high, permanently fastened in the hold.

Almost all our information on these different types of vessel has come from the skilled and valuable work of underwater archaeologists.

This French ship has been specially fitted out for underwater archaeologists and all their sophisticated equipment.

Before the research of underwater archaeologists, all we knew about the ships of ancient times came from stories, carvings, and mosaics like the one shown here.

Underwater archaeology demands a careful, step-by-step examination of any wreck, using scientific equipment.

Underwater thieves

The wrecks that have been examined carried a great variety of cargoes. A Roman ship which sank off Sardinia was carrying a heavy load of stone columns, iron bars and lead. Another craft, now lying on the bottom of the sea off the shore of Corsica, had a hold full of olive oil and wine. A third wreck was laden with bars of tin and iron, weighing several tonnes. It sank off the French town of Hyeres. Another interesting wreck, also lying off the coast of southern France, was found to contain pieces of stone that had been specially cut to shape. They were to be used for building the walls of Marseilles.

Not all wrecks are from Roman times. Some are from the Bronze Age, such as one discovered near Cape Gelidonya off the coast of Turkey. This ship carried bronze, copper and tin. Two other Bronze Age wrecks have been located. One lies off the coast of Israel, the other is in the Bay of Lipari in Italy. By looking at all these wrecks, archaeologists have discovered what kinds of wood were used in building ships. They can also work out how the main parts of a ship were put together. But they are still unsure about the sails and rigging, for these have rotted away.

Sometimes archaeologists come across articles of great beauty or value. In 1980 a French team discovered some fine furniture. There were Greek beds from the first century BC which were plated in bronze and carved with attractive decorations. But thieves had found the wreck first and carried off the most precious articles. Gangs of such underwater pirates are continually searching the bed of the Mediterranean for treasure. They are highly organised and well equipped. They know that if they can discover a valuable wreck its contents can make them a fortune in the sale rooms of Paris, Tokyo, London or New York. Sometimes archaeologists reach the remains of a vessel on the bottom of the sea only to find that the pirates have been there first and cleared out much of the important cargo. When this happens, information about the past is lost forever, but it is very difficult to stop these pirates. Not only are they hard to find, but they operate in international waters, beyond the laws of individual countries.

The Riace warriors

On 16 August 1972 an Italian diver was exploring at a depth of 300 metres off Riace on the toe of Italy. Quite by accident he noticed a bronze shoulder sticking out of the sand on the sea bed. As he looked more closely he saw that it was part of a complete statue, and that another similar one lay in the sand nearby. They were both incredibly well preserved. Carefully the two magnificent bronze figures of naked warriors were brought to the surface and taken to a museum in Florence. Here they were cleaned and treated with preservative. Scientists believe that the life-size statues had been made in Greece in the fifth century BC, at the time of Pericles. One man is almost two metres tall, the second a little shorter. They are carved in a style known to the experts as 'severe', and they were probably made in or around Athens. They are almost the only examples we have of this type of work. There are two other statues, one found on the seabed, the other on land. But they are not in such good condition as the remarkable Riace warriors.

These storage jars or amphorae *were found in the hold of a Roman ship. They were used for carrying wine, 2,000 years ago.*

RESEARCHING THE PAST

STATUES, PAINTINGS AND POTTERY

In the ancient world art played an important part in religion and in city life. Temples and statues were made to honour the gods, and magnificent buildings and monuments showed how wealthy a city was.

Marble and bronze

The Greeks employed artists to decorate buildings, tombs and shrines with stone and bronze statues and carvings. All the famous sculptors knew each other and competed to create the finest work. Phidias was the best-known for his sculptures on the Parthenon in Athens and for his statues in gold and ivory. Praxiteles is remembered as the first man to carve nude images of the goddesses. Lysippus is famous for his portrait of Alexander the Great.

Marble was the material which most sculptors liked best. Not only is it colourful and tough, but it is also very beautiful. Marble was found all over the Aegean, but the best came from Paros. It is so clear that light can pass through a piece three and a half centimetres thick.

Sculptors also worked in bronze. They liked the colour and texture of the material, which made a change from stone and marble. Statues could be made in one of two ways. In the first, sheets of bronze were moulded over a wooden statue. The second method was more complicated. The artists called it the 'lost wax' technique. The sculptor made a clay model, then covered it with wax. On top of the wax he put another layer of clay. Molten bronze (a mixture of copper and tin) was then poured on top of the wax, between the two pieces of clay. This melted the wax and the bronze took its place between the two moulds of clay. The wax drained away through holes made in the outer casing of clay. When the bronze had set, the moulds were broken, and a bronze statue was left. Before it was completely finished it had to be cleaned up to get rid of minor blemishes. Then it was smoothed and polished to look more lifelike. A bronze statue can be left out in all weathers without fear of damage.

The Riace bronzes
These famous bronze statues were discovered in 1972 on the sea bed off the town of Riace.

These pictures show three styles of classical architecture. On the left is Doric, the earliest and simplest design. The column in the middle, with the scrolls on the top, shows the Ionic style. On the right is the Corinthian style, which had slender columns and leafy decorations.

Roman art

The Romans copied Greek sculpture, making works of art in both stone and bronze. But they also had art forms of their own. The first of these was painting. The Romans were fine painters, and paintings were liked by people of all classes. The wealthy hired artists to decorate their homes, and tradesmen used paintings for advertising.

All sorts of subjects were painted by Roman artists: country scenes, people and gardens. Sometimes they painted the wall of a building with pillars, so that it did not look like a wall at all! This required

Greek vases

The Greeks were outstanding potters. The reason their work was so good is that they were extremely careful at every stage. They soaked carefully selected clay for a long time to make it pure. Then it was turned on a wheel. Simple articles were made in one piece, but more complicated shapes, such as the vases above, were made from several different sections. The clay might be as little as only 2 mm thick. After they had been painted, clay articles were fired in kilns. The kilns were fuelled with different types of wood.

'Black-figure' design, shown on the vase on the left, was popular in the sixth century BC. It was replaced by 'red-figure' work (right) in the next century. Roman pottery was cheaper and easier to make, but it never matched the beauty of the Greek vases which came before it.

considerable skill. The work was done by people who worked in the building trade, who were often slaves. As well as painting walls, painters also produced smaller pictures and huge wooden panels for decorating public buildings. The artists who did this sort of work were highly respected. Some of them became famous and lived comfortable lives on the earnings they received.

The second art form which the Romans developed was the mosaic. The idea of the mosaic came from the Greeks, but the Romans made it their own. Fine mosaics can be found all over the empire, especially in North Africa. They involved making up pictures from thousands of pieces of coloured stone set in cement, like a jig-saw. The picture on the right shows how detailed they could be. They were used for decorating walls as well as floors. They give us a great deal of information about all aspects of life in the Roman Empire. From a mosaic picture we can learn about Roman dress, houses, soldiers, ships – and even hairstyles.

CHRONOLOGY

BC
- 2900 — The port of Byblos founded in Phoenicia.
- 2000 — First palaces built in Crete.
- 1500 — Minoan civilisation at its height. Cuneiform alphabet appears. Mycenaean power grows.
- 1400 — Collapse of Minoan civilisation.
- 1200 — Iron first used in the countries of the eastern Mediterranean. Mycenaean power in decline.
- 1000 — Phoenician alphabet in use.
- 800 — Carthage founded. Greek alphabet appears. First settlements in Roman hills.
- 776 — Olympic Games begin. Start of Greek calendar.
- 760-650 — Etruscan civilisation flourishing. Greek colonies founded in southern Italy.
- 753 — According to legend, the date when Romulus founded Rome.
- 600 — Phoenician sailors sail round Africa.
- 640-560 — Life of Solon, Greek poet and law-giver, 'father of democracy'.
- 509 — Rome becomes a republic.
- 490 — Greeks defeat the Persians at Marathon.
- 525-456 — Life of Aeschylus, celebrated Greek actor and playwright.
- 447-432 — The Parthenon built in Athens.
- 485-425 — Life of Herodotus, the first famous Greek historian.
- 427-347 — Life of the philosopher Plato.
- 431-404 — Peloponnesian War and the collapse of Athenian power.
- 390 — Destruction of Rome by the Gauls.
- 336 — Alexander the Great comes to the throne of Macedonia, aged twenty.
- 334 — Alexander begins his conquests in the east.
- 384-322 — Life of Aristotle, Greek scholar and philosopher.
- 323 — Death of Alexander the Great in Babylon.
- 282 — Rome in control of northern and central Italy.
- 263-241 — First Punic War, Rome v Carthage.
- 287-212 — Life of Archimedes, scholar, philosopher and scientist.

- 218-201 — Hannibal invades Italy in second Punic War.
- 149-146 — Third Punic War ends with the destruction of Carthage.
- 73-71 — Spartacus leads Roman slave revolt.
- 58-51 — Conquest of Gaul by Julius Caesar.
- 44 — Julius Caesar assassinated.
- 27-14 — Rule of Augustus, the first emperor.

AD
- 79 — Mount Vesuvius erupts, burying the town of Pompeii.
- 70-80 — Colosseum built.
- 98-117 — Rule of Trajan.
- 220 — All free men in the empire granted the rights of Roman citizenship by Emperor Caracalla.
- 250-300 — First barbarian attacks in the Roman Empire.
- 306-337 — Rule of Constantine, who recognised Christianity 313. Byzantium becomes capital of Roman Empire
- 395 — Roman Empire divided between the west (Rome) and east (Constantinople).
- 410 — Destruction of Rome by the Visigoths.
- 527-565 — Rule of Justinian, Emperor of the Eastern Empire.

INDEX

Academus 36
Acropolis 28
Adriatic 46, 66
Aegean Sea 10, 28, 31, 74
Aeschylus 37, 70, 76
Africa 8, 14, 18, 76
Agamemnon 13
Alexander the Great 32, 40-41, 42, 74, 76
Alexandria 40, 41, 43
alphabet 15, 70, 76
amphorae 16, 72, 73
Antonius Pius 54
Aphrodite 34
Apollo 34
Arabia 58
Arcadius 64
Archimedes 42, 76
Aristophanes 37
Aristotle 36, 76
armour 12, 26, 31, 70
Artemis 35
Asia 8, 44, 54, 66
Asia Minor 20, 32, 40, 43, 46, 62
Aspasia 68, 69
Athena 29, 34, 50
Athens 24, 28-29, 30, 31, 32, 34, 36, 42, 44, 68, 74, 75, 76
Atlantic 16, 46, 54
Attila the Hun 65
Augustus 52, 69, 76
Aurelian 64

Baachus 50, 55
Babylon 40, 41, 76
Belisarius 66
Black Sea 32, 44, 54, 56
Bologna 20
Britian 16, 51, 54, 58
Byblos 14, 76
Byzantium 64, 66-67, 76

Caligual 52
Campania 20
Caracalla 76
Carthage 7, 8, 16-17, 18-19, 20, 50, 76
Caspian Sea 44
Celts 46-47
Christianity 64, 65, 66, 68, 76
Circus Maximus 58
Claudius 52
Cleopatra 42
Colosseum 58, 76
Constantine 64, 65, 66, 76
Constantinople 64, 66, 67, 76
Corinth 32, 50
Corsica 73
Cousteau, Jaques 72
Crete 7, 8, 10-11, 12, 76
Cyprus 8

Dalmatia 64
Darius 40
de Cubertin, Pierre 38
Delos 34, 72
Delphi 32, 34, 46
Demeter 34, 35
Dido 16
Diocletian 64
Dionysus 36, 50
Dodona 32, 34
Domitian 52
Druids 46

Egypt 10, 14, 32, 40, 42, 62, 69, 70
England 54, 62
Etruscans 8, 20-21, 22-23, 46, 48, 50, 59, 69, 76
Euripides 37, 70
Europe 8, 16, 44, 46, 65, 66, 70
Ezekiel 14

Florence 75
France 8, 16, 32, 33, 46, 63, 65, 72, 73

Galatia 46
Gaul see also France 46, 50, 51, 54, 56, 58, 62, 72, 76
Germany 46, 58, 64, 65
Gibraltar 8, 16, 70
government 24, 28, 50, 51, 52, 63
graves 12, 13, 22, 23, 35
Greece 7, 8, 10, 12, 24, 34, 38, 40, 69, 70, 75
Greek life 24-25, 26-28
Greek mythology 32, 34, 40
Greeks 8, 12, 18, 20, 36, 46, 48, 50, 62, 68, 74

Hades 34
Hadrian 54
Hannibal 18, 50, 76
Hanno 16
Hephaestus 34
Hera 34, 50
Hermes 34
Hero 43
Herodotus 44, 76
Hestia 35
Hipparchus 43
Homer 13, 70, 71
Horace 63
Hyeres 73

Iran 32
Islam 66
Israel 73
Issus 40
Italy 18, 20, 32, 42, 46, 48, 54, 65, 69, 70, 73, 75, 76

Jerusalem 14
Jublains 63
Julius Caesar 51, 52, 53, 56, 68, 76
Juno 50
Jupiter 48, 50, 53
Justinian 66, 67, 76
Jutes 65

Knossos 10-11

language 8, 32, 58, 62, 63, 71
Latin 58
Latium 20, 48
Lebanon 8, 14, 55
Libya 14, 18
Livia 69
Livy 63
London 53, 73

Macedonia 40, 41, 42, 76
Magna Graecia 32
Mallia 10
Malta 14
Marathon 28, 38, 76
Marcus Aurelius 54
Marius 53
Mark Anthony 52
Marseilles 32, 33, 72, 73
Marzabotto 20
Massilia see Marseilles
Mesopotamia 14, 40
Milan 64
Minerva 50
Minoans 10, 76
Morocco 14, 62
Mount Olympus 34
Mount Vesuvius 60, 61, 76
Muslims 67
Mycenae 12-13, 14, 24, 34, 70

Naples 72
Nero 52
North Africa 16, 62, 65, 70, 74

Octavian 52
Olympia 34, 35, 38
Olympic Games 38-39, 76
Orthodox Church 66
Ostia 54
Ostrogoths 65

Palmyra 64
Pan 34
Paris 53, 73
Paros 74
Parthenon 28, 74, 76
Pericles 68, 69, 75
Persia 28, 30, 40, 41, 76
Phaistos 10
Phidias 74
Phillip II 40
Phoenicia 7, 8, 14-15, 16, 18, 40, 48, 76
Pillars of Hercules 16
Piraeus 31
Plato 36, 76
Pliny 47
Plotina 69
Pompeii 60-61, 76
Pompey 42
Portugal 62
Poseidon 34, 35
Praxiteles 74
Priam 71
Provence 46
Punic Wars 16, 18, 50, 76
Pythagoras 36

religion 34-35
Remus 48
Riace 75
Roman army 56-57
Roman Empire 42, 52-53, 54-55, 56, 62-63, 64-65, 66, 68, 74, 76
Romans 8, 18, 46, 53, 62, 68, 74
Rome 7, 16, 20, 46, 48-49, 58, 62, 63, 66, 69, 76
Romulus 48, 76
Romulus Augustulus 64

Sahara 54
Sardinia 14, 73
Scicily 14, 42
Scotland 62
Senate 28, 50, 54, 59, 66
Servius Tullius 48
ships 7, 8, 10, 14, 16, 31, 33, 50, 54, 72, 73
Sicily 32, 50, 70
Socrates 28, 36, 70
Solomon 14, 67
Sophocles 37
Spain 10, 14, 16, 32, 46, 54, 62, 65, 72
Sparta 24, 28, 30, 42, 69
Syracuse 32, 42
Syria 8, 10, 15, 32, 40, 42, 62
Scythians 44-45

Tacitus 63
Tarquin the Proud 48
Thales 36
theatre 36-37, 66
Theodosius 64
Theseus 10
Tiberius 52
Titus 52
trade 7, 8, 10, 14, 16, 28, 46, 59, 71, 72
Trajan 54, 58, 69, 76
Troy 13, 48, 70, 71
Tunisia 14, 16, 53
Turkey 43, 64, 67, 71, 73
Tuscany 20

Ulysses 70, 71

Vandals 65
Vespasian 53, 63
Virgil 16, 48, 63
Visigoths 64, 65, 76

writing 7, 11, 15, 20, 48, 70

Zeus 34, 35, 38, 50

77

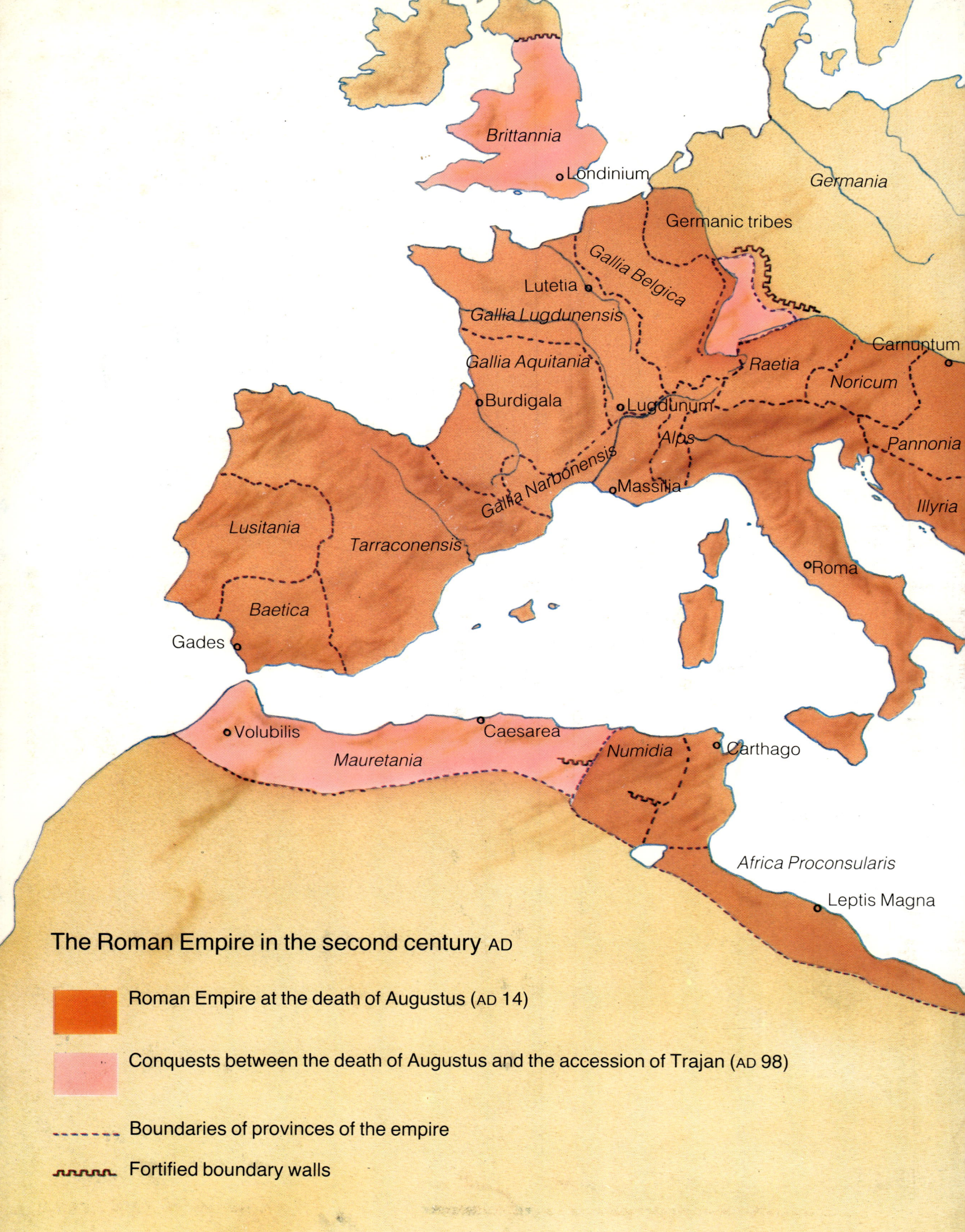